Teaching Resources E
Unit Four: Drama

to accompany

Adventures in Appreciation

ATHENA EDITION

HOLT, RINEHART AND WINSTON
Harcourt Brace & Company

Austin · New York · Orlando · Chicago · Atlanta · San Francisco · Boston · Dallas · Toronto · London

AUDIO-VISUAL CENTER
MISSOURI SOUTHERN STATE COLLEGE

Copyright © 1996 by Holt, Rinehart and Winston, Inc.

All rights reserved. No part of this publication may be reproduced or transmitted in any form or by any means, electronic or mechanical, including photocopy, recording, or any information storage and retrieval system, without permission in writing from the publisher.

Permission is hereby granted to reproduce the Worksheet Copymasters in this publication in complete pages for instructional use and not for resale by any teacher using ADVENTURES IN LITERATURE.

Printed in the United States of America

ISBN 0-03-095459-2

1 2 3 4 5 6 7 8 9   082   99 98 97 96 95 94

Acknowledgments

For permission to reprint copyrighted material, grateful acknowledgment is made to the following sources:

Robert Anderson: From *I Never Sang for My Father* by Robert Anderson. Copyright © 1966, 1968 and renewed © 1994 by Robert Anderson.

Samuel French, Inc.: Act III, Scene 2 from "Shore Acres" from *Shore Acres & Other Plays* by James A. Herne, revised and edited by Mrs. James A. Herne. Copyright © 1928 by Katherine C. Herne; copyright renewed © 1956 by John T. Herne.

Harcourt Brace & Company: From "Antigone" from *Sophocles: The Oedipus Cycle, An English Version* by Dudley Fitts and Robert Fitzgerald. Copyright 1939 by Harcourt Brace & Company; copyright renewed © 1967 by Dudley Fitts and Robert Fitzgerald.

Lorrimer Publishing Limited: From *The Third Man*, a film by Graham Greene and Carol Reed. Copyright © 1968 by Graham Greene.

TABLE OF CONTENTS

UNIT FOUR: DRAMA

DRAMA
Teacher's Notes 1
Selection Test 4

VINT David Mamet
Teacher's Notes 3
Selection Test 4

ANTIGONE Sophocles
Teacher's Notes 6
Reading Check 12
Study Guide 13
Language Skills A 18
Language Skills B 21
Building Vocabulary A 24
Building Vocabulary B 25
Selection Vocabulary Test 27
Selection Test 28

JULIUS CAESAR, Introduction and Act One
William Shakespeare
Teacher's Notes 30
Reading Check 34
Study Guide 36
Language Skills 56
Building Vocabulary 41
Selection Vocabulary Test 44
Selection Test 45

JULIUS CAESAR, Act Two William Shakespeare
Teacher's Notes 47
Reading Check 50
Study Guide 52
Language Skills 56
Building Vocabulary 59
Selection Vocabulary Test 60
Selection Test 72

JULIUS CAESAR, Act Three *William Shakespeare*

Teacher's Notes 61
Reading Check 64
Study Guide 66
Language Skills 89
Building Vocabulary 70
Selection Vocabulary Test 93
Selection Test 72

JULIUS CAESAR, Act Four *William Shakespeare*

Teacher's Notes 74
Reading Check 76
Study Guide 77
Language Skills 89
Building Vocabulary 80
Selection Vocabulary Test 93
Selection Test 94

JULIUS CAESAR, Act Five *William Shakespeare*

Teacher's Notes 81
Reading Check 84
Study Guide 86
Language Skills 89
Building Vocabulary 91
Selection Vocabulary Test 93
Selection Test 94

I NEVER SANG FOR MY FATHER *Robert Anderson*

Teacher's Notes 96
Reading Check A 104
Reading Check B 106
Study Guide A 108
Study Guide B 112
Language Skills 116
Building Vocabulary A 119
Building Vocabulary B 120
Selection Vocabulary Test 122
Selection Test 123

THE THIRD MAN *Graham Greene and Carol Reed*

Teacher's Notes 125
Reading Check 129
Study Guide 130
Language Skills 134
Building Vocabulary 138
Selection Vocabulary Test 139
Selection Test 140

UNIT ASSESSMENT STRATEGIES

    Teacher's Notes 142
    Mastery Test A 145
    Mastery Test B 148
    Analogy Test A 151
    Analogy Test B 153
    Composition Test 155

TO THE TEACHER

This booklet, *Teaching Resources E,* contains unit and selection teaching suggestions as well as a wide variety of materials that can be used to enliven instruction, address specific curriculum concerns, attend to individual student needs, and monitor student mastery.

SELECTION TEACHING MATERIALS

Teaching Notes with Answer Keys—Teaching suggestions and useful instructional features are found on the **Teacher's Notes** pages that are provided for almost every individual literary selection. The **Teacher's Notes** for a specific selection may contain a variety of the following features:
- itemized **Objectives** for teaching the selection
- an **Introduction** to the selection, with helpful background details about the author, the literary period, or the literary work
- critical or scholarly **Commentary** about the selection
- a **Reading/Critical Thinking Strategies** feature to lead students into, through, and beyond the meaning of the literary selection
- a list of **Vocabulary** words from the selection that are defined in the glossary in the textbook, along with the textbook page number or the poem line number on which each word is to be found
- a **Vocabulary Activity** to support study of the selection and development of the student's vocabulary skills

In addition to these features, the **Teacher's Notes** pages contain **Answer Keys** to worksheets that are provided to support study of a particular selection.

Copying Masters/Student Worksheets—These worksheets and support materials may include a variety of the following types of copying masters:
- **Reading Check** worksheets—provide comprehensive questions that help confirm student understanding of the meaning of the selection
- **Study Guide** worksheets—contain a series of leading questions that guide students through a close analytical reading of the selection
- **Language Skills** worksheets—contain exercises that often use brief excerpts from the literary selection to integrate grade-level-appropriate language, grammar, usage, and mechanics skills
- **Building Vocabulary** worksheets—offer a range of strategies to help students acquire vocabulary-improvement skills
- **Selection Vocabulary Tests**—provide a check of student mastery of the vocabulary words found in the selection
- **Selection Tests**—help to evaluate student understanding of the literary selection

UNIT TEACHING MATERIALS

Support materials for assessing unit mastery may include the following copying masters:
- **Mastery Tests**—provide for a comprehensive assessment of selections included in a unit or in a specific literary period
- **Analogy Lessons**—give students an opportunity to practice analyzing the kinds of relationships that may be expressed in analogies
- **Analogy Tests**—help students gain proficiency in analyzing and solving analogy problems
- **Composition Tests**—offer a choice of writing prompts that call for the student to give a developed and thoughtful written response

TEACHER'S NOTES
UNIT 4: Drama

Text Page 473

UNIT OBJECTIVES

The aims of this unit are for the student:
- To demonstrate recognition of two major categories of drama established by the Greeks—comedy and tragedy
- To identify and analyze major characteristics of drama and its particular forms
- To analyze and interpret two tragedies
- To analyze and interpret two contemporary dramas
- To use accepted criteria to evaluate an example of a dramatization of a short story
- To apply the elements of drama to the selections in this unit
- To identify specific details relevant to plot, characters and their motives, sequence of events, and settings
- To analyze and interpret passages, themes, plots, conflicts, and characters in selected dramas
- To identify a tragic hero
- To determine the tone and mood of selected dramas
- To employ charts and lists to analyze and identify characters, settings, and elements of a drama
- To identify techniques and stylistic characteristics of drama
- To compare and contrast characters in dramas
- To cite and analyze dialogue important to the dramas
- To identify the philosophies of Stoicism and idealism in selected dramas
- To recite a selected passage from a drama
- To identify and interpret the use of metaphor, puns, symbolism, and irony in selected dramas
- To identify and analyze the use of blank verse and dramatic structure in selected dramas
- To write essays analyzing and comparing and contrasting characters, themes, images, translations, and historical accounts of selected dramas
- To demonstrate an understanding of vocabulary words by solving analogies and other word problems
- To list and determine the meaning of selected words used in context
- To write a persuasive essay

OVERVIEW OF THE UNIT

For centuries drama has been the most popular of all art forms. In part, this has been so because drama involves us in a complete experience—one close to life itself. Each time the curtain goes up, actors call forth responses from an audience that may run the entire gamut of human emotions.

Be sure that students who read and study the plays in this anthology realize that the play does not exist on the pages of the book; here we simply have copies of one aspect of each play—the dialogue. Each play truly exists only when it is enacted; even then it lasts only briefly and is never repeated in exactly the same way. The unique theater experience cannot be duplicated in a classroom; it is dependent upon many variables that are not completely predictable.

There are two distinct categories of drama—tragedy and comedy. Degrees of each have come to be called by other names. Within comedy, we have farce, light comedy, situation comedy, satiric comedy, romantic comedy, and so on. We even have something called tragicomedy. The simplest way to distinguish between tragedy and comedy is to say that a tragedy has an unhappy ending and a comedy has a happy one, though this distinction does not always hold. Another distinction between the forms is the kinds of characters found in tragedy and comedy. Simply put, the greatest tragedies—the classical Greek and Shakespearean tragedies—trace the fall of someone whose stature is greater than that of the ordinary person. Comedy, on the other

continued

hand, often depicts behavior that is "below" what we consider normal or ordinary. In comedies we find such stock characters as the misanthropes, the misers, the hypocrites, the blocking parents, and so on.

You might note that if comedy is pushed too far, it can become tragic in a sense. For example, suppose a person slips on a banana peel. The audience will laugh. But suppose the victim does not move. The audience changes its attitude. It becomes solemn; it no longer laughs.

This unit begins by giving students guidelines for reading drama through a close reading of David Mamet's one-act play *Vint*. Then it moves to Sophocles' fifth-century B.C. tragedy *Antigone* followed by Shakespeare's *Julius Caesar*. To give students a taste of modern theater, Robert Anderson's realistic drama about ordinary family life, *I Never Sang for My Father*, and the film play *The Third Man* by Graham Greene and Carol Reed are included. These widely diverse selections will provide students with an opportunity to see clearly the contrast in characters and language between early and modern-day drama and will introduce them to several dramatic forms.

Throughout the unit, students are required to apply what they understand of *plot, characterization, theme, symbol, figurative language,* and *irony*. If they need reinforcement of any of these concepts, refer them to the discussions in the **Literary Terms and Techniques** section in the textbook.

TEACHER'S NOTES

VINT *David Mamet*   Text Page 480

OBJECTIVES The aims of this close-reading lesson are for the student:
- To demonstrate the ability to examine a play in depth
- To demonstrate the ability to follow a close reading and analysis of *Vint*
- To identify the elements that work together in a play
- To analyze the interdependence of the elements of a play

ANSWER KEY

SELECTION TEST

1. c
2. b
3. d
4. a
5. c
6. c
7. a
8. a
9. d
10. c

Selection Test

NAME _____

CLASS _____ DATE _____ SCORE _____

DRAMA

Introduction   (Page 474)

Reading Comprehension.   Write the letter of the *best* answer to each question.
(10 points each)

1. In the history of drama, the early Greek plays began as
   a. campfire stories of the hunt
   b. verses based on family histories
   c. enactments of religious celebrations
   d. enactments based on the lives of royalty   1. _____

2. The form of drama most often associated with Italy is
   a. social satire   c. intellectual theater
   b. grand opera   d. musical comedy   2. _____

3. The strolling minstrels who roamed the marketplaces and fairs appeared in
   a. the twentieth century   c. classical Greece
   b. the seventeenth century   d. the Middle Ages   3. _____

4. The terms *tragedy* and *comedy* were established by the
   a. Greeks   c. French
   b. Romans   d. Italians   4. _____

5. The voice over and the dissolve are dramatic conventions that belong to
   a. Elizabethan drama   c. screenplays
   b. French farce   d. Greek tragedy   5. _____

6. What does Mamet suggest about bureaucratic officials by reducing them to playing cards?
   a. That they are as important as members of a royal court
   b. That their function is to control the lives of others
   c. That their function is to outsmart each other
   d. That they are important in title only, with no real power   6. _____

7. Commissioner Persolin's attitude upon first learning that his clerks are still at work is
   a. pride in the clerks
   b. anger at the clerks
   c. curiosity over the situation
   d. indifference toward the clerks   7. _____

8. The change in Persolin's attitude toward the clerks when he discovers that he is the ace of clubs signifies that he
   a. can be persuaded by flattery
   b. really wasn't angry in the first place
   c. can be persuaded by reason
   d. cannot be persuaded by flattery   8. _____

continued

4   Teaching Resources E   •   *Adventures in Appreciation*

NAME _____

CLASS _____ DATE _____   SELECTION TEST—CONTINUED

9. The tone of most plays is best described as
   a. the same throughout the play   c. always comic
   b. always somber   d. varying throughout the play   9. _____

10. The opening lines of *Vint* give all of the following information *except*
    a. where the play takes place
    b. why the commissioner has returned to his office
    c. why the clerks are still at the office
    d. who Persolin is   10. _____

Teaching Resources E • *Adventures in Appreciation*

TEACHER'S NOTES

ANTIGONE *Sophocles* Text Page 494

OBJECTIVES The aims of this lesson are for the student:
- To identify specific details relevant to the plot and main characters of *Antigone*
- To identify the cause of conflict in *Antigone*
- To analyze characters in the Greek drama *Antigone*
- To explain the roles of the chorus in *Antigone*
- To determine the meanings of the odes presented within *Antigone*
- To tell in one's own words the themes presented throughout *Antigone*
- To identify the tragic figure in *Antigone*
- To analyze the characteristics and conflicts of the tragic figure in *Antigone*
- To determine the relationships between words in selected analogies using synonyms and antonyms
- To write a brief essay using a statement from *Antigone* to support an opinion
- To write an opinion statement on a national or local issue

SUMMARY/ INTRODUCTION The plot of this tragedy is simple. The play begins after a war, in which Oedipus' sons, Polyneices and Eteocles, battle over the throne of Thebes and slay each other. Creon decrees that Eteocles, the brother who died defending his country, be buried as a hero with full military honors. Polyneices, the brother who sought to overthrow Creon's government, will be left to rot—unburied, prey to birds and scavenging dogs. The two remaining children of Oedipus, Ismene and Antigone, are horrified over Creon's ruling because it defies religious laws. However, Ismene does not wish to disobey her uncle. Antigone, on the other hand, does intend to defy him and bury Polyneices (Prologue).

The news that someone has attempted to bury Polyneices' body is brought to Creon by a Sentry. Note here how Creon seems to strike fear into those around him. When the Chorus of elders comments on the possibility that the gods themselves might have covered the body, Creon shouts, "Intolerable!" (page 501; line 96). Why would the gods look upon Polyneices with favor? He had tried to loot their temples, burn their images, destroy the state. But Creon knows that there are men whose purpose would be served by covering the body; it would be an act of defiance against existing authority, already in a shaky position because of the war (Scene 1).

The Sentry returns with Antigone, claiming he found her crying over the prince's body as she sprinkled dust and wine over it. Antigone confesses to Creon that she *has* broken his law. She does not defy him with triumph, but with her head lowered. She tells Creon that there is a higher law than his, which demands that she bury her brother; she will abide by this higher law, though it means her own death (Scene 2).

It is interesting at this point to note the comment of the Chorus. "Like father, like daughter: both headstrong, deaf to reason!/She has never learned to yield" (page 507; lines 75–76). Antigone is Oedipus' daughter, and she will not yield. She continues to argue that a brother is a brother. In death the brothers are equal, and both deserve respect and burial. It is unimportant that one brother died defending his country and the other died a traitor. "Which of us can say what the gods hold wicked?" she says to Creon (page 508; line 116).

Creon sends for Ismene, intending to punish her as well as Antigone. Ismene is guilty by knowledge, if not by deed. But Antigone is proud. She will not beg for her life, and she does not wish to "share" this moment of glory in death with her sister. Haimon enters to discuss the situation with his father. Antigone and Haimon are betrothed—thus Antigone is linked to Creon not only through her mother, but also through Creon's own son. The young prince tries to explain to his father that it would be wise to bury Polyneices. Such a decision would strengthen Creon's position as king—Haimon knows that the people are on Antigone's side, that Creon's temper

continued

terrifies them. But Creon will not, cannot, understand that his laws are not absolute. Creon sees a change of mind as a sign of weakness. If he cannot obey his own laws, how can he expect anyone else to have faith in his government (Scene 3)?

(A question might arise with the introduction of Haimon: students will want to know how it is possible that Antigone and Haimon can marry, since they are first cousins. Explain that such a marriage would not have been considered unusual at the time of the play.)

Unable to kill Antigone directly, Creon decrees that she be closed up in a burial vault (Scene 4).

Creon is next visited by the blind prophet Teiresias, who prophesies that the time is not far off when Creon will pay back corpse for corpse; for his crime of thrusting a child of this world into "living night," he will be punished (page 524). Creon now finally admits that, though it is hard to give in, it is worse to risk everything for stubborn pride. He orders Antigone to be freed (Scene 5).

But Antigone has hanged herself. Haimon, discovering her body, turns on his father and narrowly misses him with a sword. Haimon then drives the sword into his own side and dies. Creon's wife, discovering that her son has died, also kills herself. Creon has changed his mind too late (Exodos).

There is something unusual about this play: it is entitled *Antigone*, but Antigone does not seem to be the main character; in fact, she disappears halfway through the action. The play seems to pivot around Creon; the burden of making judgments is his, not Antigone's. To Antigone, there is no choice: she must bury her brother. However, Creon doesn't really seem central to the play from beginning to end either. Ask students at the end of the reading if they think the play should have been titled *Creon*.

READING/CRITICAL THINKING STRATEGIES

Analyzing Plot

As a prereading strategy for *Antigone*, you might define *dilemma* for students and ask them to consider choices that people sometimes have to make that involve dilemmas. Tell students that many of the conflicts in this play involve dilemmas. As students read this section of the play, have them determine which parts of the play provide important background information and which parts serve to establish a dilemma. You may want to ask students to speculate on the best way to resolve the conflict. Students might complete a chart like the one below. After students have completed their reading, ask them to discuss their findings. What do they see as the most important conflict?

Exposition	Conflict and Issues Involved
Curse of Oedipus	
Brother is dead	

Making Inferences About Character: Analyzing Character

Before students begin reading Scene 1 of *Antigone*, remind them that in drama an audience has to make inferences about a character based upon the character's words and actions. The audience may also make some inferences based on what other characters in the play say about the character. Tell students that as they read, they should pay particular attention to what Creon's speeches and the speeches of others reveal about his character. Students may benefit from keeping a chart like the one on page 8. When the class has finished reading, ask students to compare their findings and then to discuss whether they think Creon is a good ruler.

continued

Inference	Evidence
Has potential to be a good leader	The Choragos considers the beginning of his reign auspicious.

Expressing an Opinion

As a prereading strategy for Scene 2 of *Antigone*, ask students to consider how the characters and values of Antigone and Creon differ. Tell students that as they read this scene they should consider Antigone's motives and Creon's motives. How much of their conflict arises from their values? How much from their personalities? Students might map or prepare a cluster diagram of their ideas. After students have finished their reading, ask them to share their findings and to express an opinion about the sources of conflict between Antigone and Creon.

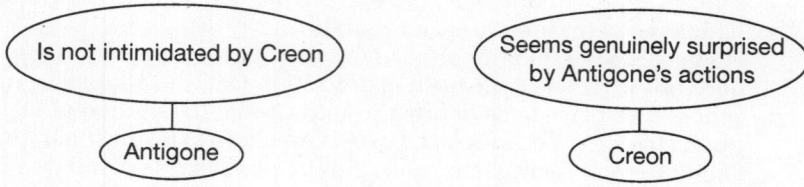

Analyzing Conflicts

Before students begin reading Scene 3 of *Antigone*, ask students to discuss the idea of *loyalty*. To whom do we owe loyalty? To our country? To our government? (Is there a difference between the two?) To our parents? To ourselves? How should the decision be made if we have to choose among them? Tell students that as they read this scene they should consider the choices that the characters have to make. What issues or values are involved in those choices? After students have finished reading, ask them to discuss their findings. Encourage them to discuss the complexities of the issues.

Arguments/Values	Comments/Reactions
Creon argues that law and order are essential to society.	The family is the basic unit of society, but Creon seems rigid.
Creon sees women as inferior to men.	

Expressing an Opinion

Before students begin reading Scene 4 of *Antigone*, you might ask them to comment on the idea that our lives may be predetermined. For example, do students believe that a person has an appointed time to die? Remind students of the Greek belief in the role of fate. You may want to have them review the play to find all the references to fate so far. Tell students that as they read this portion of the play they should decide whether or not Sophocles believed that fate is what determines the characters' actions. After students have finished their reading, ask them to express and support their opinions.

Analyzing Character

Before students begin reading Scene 5 of "Antigone," you might ask them to discuss what inferences they have made about Creon to this point. Tell students that as they read this portion of the play, they should consider each of Creon's arguments and decisions. Why does he do what he does? After students have completed their reading, ask them to share their findings and to discuss their reactions to Creon's character and decisions.

continued

Argument/Decision	Reason	Reaction
Teiresias and Creon argue.	Teiresias believes Creon has defied the gods, but Creon's pride will not let him see Teiresias' point.	

Synthesizing

As a prereading strategy for the Exodos of *Antigone,* ask students to summarize the action so far. What questions of values have been raised? (Duty to gods vs. duty to state, duty to family vs. other duties, fate vs. free will, and so on.) You may want to list their responses on the chalkboard. Tell students that as they read this portion of the play they should consider whether or not this play offers any insight into how these issues should be resolved. Can these issues be resolved neatly or are they dilemmas? Why do students think this play has remained popular with audiences for centuries? Do students think the play is valuable for readers today? Why or why not? After students have completed their reading, ask them to share their findings. What do students think is the most important question the play raises? Can this question be answered?

VOCABULARY

The following words are defined in the glossary (the number in parentheses indicates the page where the word first appears).

decree	(495)	lithe	(503)	blasphemy	(518)
carrion	(495)	yoke	(503)	lament (ation)	(518)
crest	(497)	sultry	(503)	dirge (s)	(518)
sate (d)	(497)	deflect (s)	(503)	transgress	(519)
garland	(497)	expansive (ly)	(504)	profane (d)	(520)
auspicious	(498)	edict	(505)	untrammeled	(521)
counsel	(498)	mortal	(505)	entrails	(521)
scavenge (–ing)	(499)	insolent (–ence)	(507)	welter	(521)
comprehensive	(499)	brazen	(507)	defile	(523)
impassive (ly)	(500)	transcend (s)	(511)	synthetic	(523)
intolerable	(501)	deference	(511)	citadel	(525)
senile	(502)	subordinate	(511)	crevice	(527)
demoralize (–ing)	(502)	seduce	(513)		
furrow (s)	(503)	absolve	(516)		

ANSWER KEYS

READING CHECK

A.
1. T
2. T
3. F
4. T
5. T
6. F
7. F
8. F
9. T
10. F

B. Answers may vary. Students should list the following major events: Antigone buries her brother Polyneices against Creon's orders. Creon has Antigone locked in a tomb, where she hangs herself. Haimon finds her body and kills himself. Stricken with grief for her son, Eurydice kills herself, cursing Creon.

continued

STUDY GUIDE

1. For seasonal festivals to honor the god Dionysos
2. (a) All the actors were men. (b) The actors wore large masks and oversized costumes, including boots with raised soles to make them taller. (c) Plays included a chorus, whose fifteen members chanted their lines in unison.
3. In their fight for the throne, Creon sided with Eteocles over Polyneices, who then went into exile, raised an army, and returned to storm the city's gates. Creon thus views Polyneices as a traitor.
4. **a.** Antigone's burial of Polyneices' body; the deaths in the cavern of Antigone and Haimon; Eurydice's suicide
   b. Sophocles sends eyewitnesses onto the stage as the characters of the sentry and the messenger, who proceed to describe in detail what has occurred.
5. (a) From the very beginning, Antigone anticipates her inevitable death if she defies Creon and buries Polyneices; lines such as 56–57 and 80–81 on page 496 already point to her death. (b) After being detained for her actions, Antigone accepts her fate calmly, refuses to seek forgiveness, and speaks even righteously of the death decreed for her (page 505). (c) Haimon states unequivocally: "Then she must die." (page 515, line 119). (d) The ominous prophecy of Teiresias, never known by the Chorus to have been wrong, erases any doubt that misfortune can somehow be averted.
6. **a.** Creon represents the position that full obedience to the law of the land is of the utmost importance in maintaining an orderly society. He believes that there is no greater evil than anarchy (page 513, line 42). Antigone, however, recognizes a higher authority—that of God. "The immortal unrecorded laws of God/ . . . shall be,/Operative forever, beyond man utterly" (page 505, lines 61–63). This is a matter of duty versus conscience, of loyalty to one's country versus loyalty to one's most deeply held values. Antigone's defiance of civil law and the other characters' reactions to it form the crux of the play.
   b. Antigone is strong-willed, defiant, determined in her desire to bury her brother properly, following the dictates of the gods above those of Creon. Ismene is fearful, weak, unable to disobey laws that were intended for the public good (page 496, line 63).
   c. Creon expects Haimon to obey him not only as his subject, but as his son, saying that a man prays for sons that are attentive and dutiful in his house (page 511, Scene 3, lines 13–14). Haimon, however, is torn between his love and respect for Creon, and his love for Antigone, in the end turning against his father.
7. Oedipus, by killing his father and marrying his mother, has brought upon his family a curse not broken by his own death. Basic to the play is the sense that Antigone, as Oedipus' daughter, is doomed to suffer a terrible fate because of him.
8. As leader of the Chorus of elders, Choragos can be assumed to be a wise statesman whose comments should be taken seriously. He is a relatively impartial barometer by which to judge right and wrong, wisdom and folly. Thus, as he seems to sanction the king's edict (page 499, lines 39–40; page 513, lines 49–50; page 518, lines 45–46), then finds elements of truth in both Creon's and Haimon's arguments (page 514, lines 92–94), then advises releasing Antigone, the audience tends to accept his point of view.
9. The destruction of Creon and his family, and particularly the final lines of Choragos, indicate that Antigone has been proved correct.
10. **a.** He was repulsed before he was fully satisfied, before he was glutted with his enemies' blood.
    b. He calls it favorable, or seeming to bode well, because Thebes has been victorious and the war is over. Of course, Creon's very first decree, about to be announced, will bring untold suffering, hardly an auspicious beginning.
    c. He was calm, not showing emotion.
    d. Flexible, supple
    e. Answers will vary, but students might suggest a gymnast or a dancer.
    f. By giving in to Creon's wishes, by not going against his will
    g. She was not confined or restrained in any way.
11. Answers will vary. Most students will probably agree that Creon is a proud and stubborn man whose refusal to bend in the manner suggested by Haimon causes his ruin.
12. **a.** Responses will vary.
    b. Responses will vary.

LANGUAGE SKILLS A

A. 1. Eteocles
   2. a sweet . . . food
   3. Stoning . . . square

continued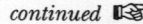

4. death . . . honor
5. their commander
6. No tender . . . power
7. brothers . . . blood
8. Stiff-necked anarchists
9. Antigone

B. 10. Answers will vary, but students should see that appositives can help introduce persons or events.

C. Answers will vary. Suggested answers follow.
11. Creon, Menoikeus' son, is the new king of Thebes.
12. Polyneices, the son of Oedipus, attacked his own city.
13. One of the sentries, the corporal, noticed the burial dust.
14. The Choragos wonders why the princess Antigone has been taken captive.
15. Creon accuses Antigone of a double insolence, breaking the law and then boasting of it.

D. 16.–20. Sentences will vary.

LANGUAGE SKILLS B

A. 1. as his father does his
2. like that
3. like a boy now
4. than a man can
5. as here you have made bright anger/strike between father and son
6. like the voice of death
7. as any grave
8. like yours
9. as I see for others
10. as I do
11. than any baseness
12. than this
13. than I can bear

B. 14.–17. Explanations will vary.

C. 18.–24. Comparisons will vary.

BUILDING VOCABULARY A

1. decree
2. comprehensive
3. intolerable
4. garland
5. auspicious
6. sated
7. scavenge (or scavenged)
8. impassive
9. furrows
10. senile

BUILDING VOCABULARY B

Answers will vary. Possible answers for some items are given here.

1. A person might always address the President as "Mr. President" in the conversation, ask questions politely, be careful not to interrupt the President's comments, and so on.
2. High cholesterol has been strongly connected to the occurrence of heart disease.
6. Human entrails include the heart, lungs, liver, large and small intestines, stomach, etc.
8. Volcanoes are the result of crevices in the earth's crust that allow molten rock, gases, and hot ash to push up to the earth's surface. Volcanic eruptions are sometimes accompanied by earthquakes that may create huge crevices in the ground. As it cools, hot ash from volcanoes often forms a surface with many crevices.

SELECTION VOCABULARY TEST

A. 1. e   6. k
2. h   7. f
3. a   8. c
4. j   9. i
5. b   10. d

B. 1. b   4. b
2. a   5. d
3. c

SELECTION TEST

A. 1. a   4. b
2. d   5. b
3. c

B. 6. b   9. d
7. b   10. b
8. a

Reading Check

NAME _____

CLASS _____ DATE _____ SCORE _____

DRAMA

Antigone *Sophocles* (Page 494)

───────── **READING CHECK** ─────────

A. True/False. Write **T** for a true statement. Write **F** for a false statement.

_____ 1. Creon has refused to bury Polyneices because Polyneices has attacked the city and is seen as a traitor.

_____ 2. Antigone wants to bury her brother because the laws of the gods demand it.

_____ 3. Ismene helps her sister bury their brother.

_____ 4. Creon says that he values the state more than he values private friendship.

_____ 5. Because she attempts to bury her brother, Antigone is sentenced to death.

_____ 6. Ismene is also sentenced to die with her sister.

_____ 7. Antigone begs Creon to save her life and begs forgiveness for disobeying his law.

_____ 8. Haimon fully supports his father in condemning Antigone to death.

_____ 9. Teiresias begs Creon to change his mind and allow the burial.

_____ 10. Creon finally gives in, Antigone is saved, and the play ends happily.

B. List the major events in the play in the order in which they occurred.

_____
_____
_____
_____
_____
_____
_____
_____
_____
_____

Study Guide

NAME _____
CLASS _____ DATE _____ SCORE _____

Drama

ANTIGONE   (Pages 489–534)

Sophocles (496?–406 B.C.)

Understanding the Writer and His Background

1. For what occasions did Sophocles probably write his plays?
   _____

2. Name at least three aspects of ancient Greek theater that differ markedly from modern drama.
   _____
   _____
   _____

Understanding the Play

3. Why does Creon forbid the proper burial of Polyneices? _____
   _____
   _____

4. Most of the major action in this play takes place offstage.

   a. What are three events that occur offstage? _____
      _____
      _____

   b. How does Sophocles incorporate these events into the play? How does the audience learn about them? _____
      _____
      _____

continued

Teaching Resources E • *Adventures in Appreciation*   13

NAME _____

CLASS _____ DATE _____ STUDY GUIDE—CONTINUED

5. There is very little real suspense in this play. Find at least two separate places where Sophocles provides strong indications that the drama will not end happily.

_____
_____
_____
_____
_____
_____
_____

6. The essence of drama is conflict. Describe the following conflicts in *Antigone*:

   a. Between civil law and divine law: _____
   _____
   _____
   _____
   _____
   _____
   _____

   b. Between Antigone and Ismene: _____
   _____
   _____
   _____

continued

NAME _____

CLASS _____ DATE _____ STUDY GUIDE—CONTINUED

    c. Between Creon and Haimon: _____
_____
_____
_____
_____

7. Oedipus is already dead when the play begins. Explain how he continues to exert a strong influence.
_____
_____
_____
_____
_____

8. Describe the function of Choragos. Explain how he has a strong influence in molding audience reaction.
_____
_____
_____
_____
_____
_____
_____
_____

9. Whose viewpoint—Creon's or Antigone's—does Sophocles suggest is correct?
_____
_____
_____
_____

continued

Teaching Resources E • *Adventures in Appreciation* 15

NAME _____

CLASS _____ DATE _____ STUDY GUIDE—CONTINUED

Understanding Vocabulary

10. Consult the glossary as needed to answer each question below:

   a. What does it mean that Polyneices was thrown back before he was *sated* with the blood of Thebes (page 497)? _____

   b. Why does Choragos call the dawn of Creon's reign *auspicious* (page 498)? Why is this ironic? _____

   c. What was Creon's manner as he waited *impassively* (page 500)? _____

   d. What are *lithe* fish (page 503)? _____

   e. What kind of person might you describe as *lithe*? _____

   f. How might Haimon show *deference* to Creon (page 511)? _____

   g. How did the woman walk *untrammeled* (page 521)? _____

continued

16 Teaching Resources E • *Adventures in Appreciation*

NAME _____

CLASS _____ DATE _____   STUDY GUIDE—CONTINUED

Understanding Literary Elements

11. The *tragic hero* of a drama is not inherently evil but brings about his downfall through a character flaw or error in judgment. Briefly explain whether you think Creon fits this definition.

_____

_____

_____

_____

_____

_____

Writing and Responding to Literature

12. Describe your personal reaction to the two major characters, both of whom were proud and stubborn but loyal to a deep conviction.

  a. Was Antigone admirable in her insistence on burying Polyneices, or was she just being foolhardy given the inevitable consequences? Explain your opinion.

  _____

  _____

  _____

  _____

  _____

  b. What is your impression of Creon at the end? Consider the following questions: Do you sympathize with him? Do you feel he deserves this fate? Will he emerge from this ordeal a more humble, tolerant man—or a broken man? Will he be able to rule Thebes effectively?

  _____

  _____

  _____

  _____

Language Skills A

NAME _____

CLASS _____ DATE _____ SCORE _____

Antigone, Prologue–Ode 2   *Sophocles*   (Page 494)

―――――――――――――― APPOSITIVES ――――――――――――――

An **appositive** is a noun or pronoun that follows another noun or pronoun to identify or explain it. Notice how appositives add clarity and more detail in this excerpt from Scene 1.

> **Creon.** . . . you never hesitated in your duty to our late ruler <u>Oedipus</u>; and when Oedipus died, your loyalty was transferred to his children. Unfortunately, as you know, his two sons, <u>the princes Eteocles and Polyneices</u>, have killed each other in battle. . . . *(Page 498)*

Adding *Oedipus* after the noun *ruler* makes it clear which late ruler Creon refers to. The underlined phrase following the noun *sons* adds information about them—their names and their royal titles. When an appositive has modifiers, as this one does, it forms an **appositive phrase.**

You may note that the appositive phrase in the excerpt is set off by commas. This punctuation indicates that the information is not really essential to identifying the sons: Oedipus must have had just these two sons.

ACTIVITY A

Underline the appositives and appositive phrases in the following quotations.

1. Creon buried our brother Eteocles/With military honors . . . *(Page 495)*
2. But his body must lie in the fields, a sweet treasure/For carrion birds to find as they search for food. *(Page 495)*
3. . . . Creon is coming here/To announce it publicly; and the penalty—/Stoning to death in the public square! *(Page 495)*
4. It will not be the worst of deaths—death without honor. *(Page 496)*
5. Polyneices their commander/Roused them with windy phrases, *(Page 497)*
6. . . . and as he turned, great Thebes—/No tender victim for his noisy power—/Rose like a dragon behind him, shouting war. *(Page 497)*
7. These two only, brothers in blood,/Face to face in matchless rage,/Mirroring each the other's death,/Clashed in long combat. *(Page 498)*
8. There have been those who have whispered together,/Stiff-necked anarchists, putting their heads together,/Scheming against me in alleys. *(Page 502)*
9. Surely this captive woman/Is the princess, Antigone. *(Page 503)*

continued ☞

18 Teaching Resources E • *Adventures in Appreciation*

NAME _____

CLASS _____ DATE _____ LANGUAGE SKILLS A—CONTINUED

ACTIVITY B

Look back over the appositives and appositive phrases in Activity A. Consider that most of them come from the very beginning of the play, the Prologue. Explain below why you think a writer would use many appositives in the opening dialogue of a play or the opening paragraphs of a story or an essay.

10. _____
_____
_____

Punctuating Appositives

If an appositive is not essential to understanding the noun or pronoun it follows, it is set off from the sentence by a comma, or two commas.

    EXAMPLE   These two only, brothers in blood, . . . *(Page 498)* (We know already who the two are.)

If an appositive is essential to understanding the preceding noun or pronoun, it is not set off with commas.

    EXAMPLE   Creon buried our brother Eteocles *(Page 495)* (They have two brothers; the appositive tells us which is meant.)

If the writer wishes to call particular attention to the content of the appositive, it is set off with one or two dashes.

    EXAMPLE   . . . the worst of deaths—death without honor. *(Page 496)*

ACTIVITY C

Combine each pair of sentences by making the second one an appositive and inserting it into the first sentence.

    EXAMPLE   Antigone wanted to bury Polyneices.

                    Antigone was one of the daughters of Oedipus.

                    Antigone, one of the daughters of Oedipus, wanted to bury Polyneices.

11. Creon is the new king of Thebes. Creon is Menoikeus' son.

_____
_____

continued

NAME _____

CLASS _____ DATE _____ LANGUAGE SKILLS A—CONTINUED

12. Polyneices attacked his own city. Polyneices was the son of Oedipus.

_____
_____

13. One of the sentries noticed the burial dust. He was the corporal.

_____
_____

14. The Choragos wonders why the princess has been taken captive. The princess is Antigone.

_____
_____

15. Creon accuses Antigone of a double insolence. The two parts of her insolence are breaking the law and then boasting of it.

_____
_____

ACTIVITY D

Write five sentences of your own, each one about a real or an imaginary person. Use an appositive phrase in each sentence to help identify or describe the person.

16. _____
_____

17. _____
_____

18. _____
_____

19. _____
_____

20. _____
_____

Language Skills B

NAME _____

CLASS _____ DATE _____ SCORE _____

Antigone, Scene 3–Exodus *Sophocles* (Page 511)

USING COMPARISONS

Writers frequently use **comparisons** to add interest and vividness to their work. Notice how comparisons make the Messenger's opinion very strong and clear in these lines from the Exodos in *Antigone*.

> **Messenger.** . . .
> Let him live <u>like a king</u> in his great house:
> If his pleasure is gone, I would not give
> So much <u>as the shadow of smoke</u> for all he owns.
> (Page 525, lines 13–15)

To "live like a king" suggests a life of ease, wealth, and power. For the Messenger, however, such a life would have no value if there were no pleasure in it. It would not even be worth "the shadow of smoke," a vivid image of something fleeting and lacking substance.

Direct comparisons are usually expressed with phrases or clauses introduced by the words *like* or *as*. Another word that signals comparison is *than*.

>   EXAMPLES   Is a woman stronger <u>than we</u>?   *(Page 513, line 48)*
>
>   Nothing is closer to me <u>than your happiness</u>.   *(Page 514, line 70)*

ACTIVITY A

Underline the direct comparison expressed in each of the following quotations.

1. Must not any son/Value his father's fortune as his father does his?   *(Page 514)*
2. A man like that, when you know him, turns out empty.   *(Page 514)*
3. Who is it that's talking like a boy now?   *(Page 515)*
4. Let him do, or dream to do, more than a man can.   *(Page 516)*
5. Surely you swerve upon ruin/The just man's consenting heart,/As here you have made bright anger/Strike between father and son—   *(Page 516)*
6. That voice is like the voice of death!   *(Page 519)*
7. A small room, still as any grave, enclosed her.   *(Page 520)*
8. But in her marriage deathless Fate found means/To build a tomb like yours for all her joy.   *(Page 521)*

continued ☞

NAME _____

CLASS _____ DATE _____   LANGUAGE SKILLS B—CONTINUED

9. My boy described it,/Seeing for me as I see for others. *(Page 521)*

10. It is for your own good that I speak as I do. *(Page 523)*

11. . . . bribes are baser than any baseness. *(Page 523)*

12. What burden worse than this shall I find there? *(Page 528)*

13. All true, all true, and more than I can bear! *(Page 528)*

Recognizing Literal and Figurative Comparisons

Literal comparisons relate things that are essentially alike, for instance, two people: "My older sister is taller *than I am.*" **Figurative** comparisons relate things that are essentially unlike: "In my eyes, my older sister stands taller *than a tree.*"

When a figurative comparison is introduced directly with *like, as,* or *than,* it is called a **simile.** Writers use similes and other forms of figurative language to provide a more vivid look at something or someone they are describing.

ACTIVITY B

Explain what descriptive words come to your mind when you read each of the underlined figurative comparisons.

EXAMPLE   Let him live <u>like a king</u> . . . *(Page 525)*

He would be very rich and powerful, having absolute authority over everyone around him.

14. Or they walk with fixed eyes, <u>as blind men walk</u>. *(Page 511)*

_____

_____

15. Who is it that's talking <u>like a boy</u> now? *(Page 515)*

_____

_____

16. That voice is <u>like the voice of death</u>! *(Page 519)*

_____

_____

_____

continued

22   Teaching Resources E   •   *Adventures in Appreciation*

17. A small room, still <u>as any grave</u>, enclosed her. *(Page 520)*

_____
_____

ACTIVITY C

Complete each sentence by adding a figurative comparison of your own. Try to avoid using clichés—overused expressions such as "cold as ice" or "hard as a rock."

18. They chattered like _____
_____

19. Watching that movie was more boring than _____
_____

20. The ruler's heart was as hard as _____
_____

21. The dancer moved like _____
_____

22. The wind blew through the trees more fiercely than _____
_____

23. Their voices were as loud and grating as _____
_____

24. After sloshing through rain-filled streets, they looked like _____
_____

Building Vocabulary A

Antigone *Sophocles* (Page 494)

───────── USING WORDS IN CONTEXT ─────────

ACTIVITY

From the following list of vocabulary words, choose the word that best completes the meaning in each sentence below. (You may need to change the word's form slightly—for example, put a verb in past tense.)

> auspicious   garland
> decree   senile
> impassive   furrow
> intolerable sate
> comprehensive scavenge

1. According to the controversial school board _____, students must wear uniforms to school.

2. Our semester exam in history was _____, covering everything from the Pilgrims' landing at Plymouth to the Civil War.

3. To the American colonists, British rule became so _____ that revolution was necessary.

4. In ancient Greece, an honored athlete often wore a _____ of laurel leaves on his head.

5. Being late for work on the first day is not a(n) _____ beginning.

6. After hours of watching late-night movies, Janine and Valencia were _____ with ads for used-car dealers and low-cost mail-order jewelry.

7. Along the roadside, children _____ for aluminum cans to redeem at the recycling center.

8. The _____ faces of the jury members gave no clue to the verdict that was about to be announced.

9. From the air, _____ in the freshly planted field appeared as long, straight lines.

10. The _____ man was sometimes unable to remember even his own name or address.

Adventures in Appreciation

Building Vocabulary B

NAME _____

CLASS _____ DATE _____ SCORE _____

Antigone *Sophocles* (Page 494)

―――――― **CREATING CONTEXT** ――――――

Sometimes you can guess the meaning of an unfamiliar word from clues in the word's **context**—the words, phrases, and sentences surrounding the unfamiliar word. You may also take hints, often without realizing it, from your personal store of knowledge—all your experience and previous reading. This "storehouse" is your *prior knowledge,* that is, what you already know.

ACTIVITY

Use your prior knowledge to create the context suggested for each italicized vocabulary word in the sentences below. Write in the space provided.

1. If you were invited to have a ten-minute private conversation with the President of the United States, what might you do to show *deference* to the nation's leader?

   _____
   _____
   _____
   _____

2. Why do nutritionists recommend that you *subordinate* high-cholesterol foods (fatty meats, etc.) to low-cholesterol foods (leafy vegetables, etc.) in your diet?

   _____
   _____
   _____
   _____

3. Snow skiers often say they feel *untrammeled* as they glide down the slopes. Describe a situation in which you experience such a feeling. _____
   _____
   _____
   _____

continued

NAME _____

CLASS _____ DATE _____ BUILDING VOCABULARY B—CONTINUED

4. Imagine that a movie script calls for a teen-ager's room that is a "*welter* of typical teen-age possessions." Describe how the room might look. _____
_____
_____

5. Looking around your classroom, name as many items as possible that are not *synthetic*.
_____
_____
_____

6. Name as many organs as you can that make up the *entrails* of humans. _____
_____
_____

7. When your high-school days are over, what are some things you will *lament* as left behind forever from your daily life? _____
_____
_____
_____

8. From your own knowledge of science, describe how the word *crevice* relates to volcanoes.
_____
_____
_____
_____

Selection Vocabulary Test

NAME _____

CLASS _____ DATE _____ SCORE _____

Antigone   *Sophocles*   (Page 494)

---------- VOCABULARY TEST ----------

A. Match each word in column I with the correct definition in column II. Place the letter of each definition you choose in the space provided. (5 points each)

I	II
_____ 1. decree	a. the peak or highest point
_____ 2. carrion	b. a wreath of flowers
_____ 3. crest	c. shameless
_____ 4. sate	d. showing no emotion
_____ 5. garland	e. an official order
_____ 6. auspicious	f. a private thought; a secret
_____ 7. counsel	g. intense heat
_____ 8. brazen	h. rotten or decaying
_____ 9. comprehensive	i. including all necessary details
_____ 10. impassive	j. to satisfy to the fullest extent
	k. favorable; boding well

B. In the space provided, write the letter of the word or phrase closest in meaning to the italicized word. (10 points each)

_____ 1. The television station reported on the *intolerable* conditions in the apartment building.
(a) ideal   (b) unbearable   (c) interesting   (d) humid

_____ 2. The captain's orders served to *demoralize* the entire company.
(a) corrupt   (b) inspire   (c) calm   (d) help

_____ 3. The broken wires fell in a *welter* at the foot of the building.
(a) deep pool   (b) mud puddle   (c) jumbled mass   (d) ditch

_____ 4. The country-western singer *lamented* the loss of his sweetheart.
(a) celebrated   (b) mourned   (c) recognized   (d) sang of

_____ 5. She spoke of her competitor with *malice*.
(a) glee   (b) fear   (c) sadness   (d) spite

Teaching Resources E • Adventures in Appreciation

Selection Test

NAME _____

CLASS _____ DATE _____ SCORE _____

DRAMA

Antigone Sophocles *(Page 494)*

AN OPEN-BOOK TEST

A. Reading Comprehension. Write the letter of the *best* answer to each question. *(10 points each)*

1. The main antagonists in the play are
   a. Creon and Antigone
   b. Creon and the State
   c. Creon and his conscience
   d. Haimon and his father   1. _____

2. The Prologue and Chorus furnish much background information, including all of the following *except*
   a. the outcome of the siege of Thebes
   b. how Antigone's brothers perished
   c. how Antigone's parents died
   d. how Creon has become ruler of Thebes   2. _____

3. Creon's decree that Polyneices shall not be buried is
   a. in accord with Greek religious practices
   b. popular with most Theban citizens
   c. rejected by Antigone as a violation of a divine law
   d. Creon's way of punishing Antigone   3. _____

4. Scene 3, which begins on a note of respect and submission, ends with Haimon's
   a. threatening to kill his father
   b. complete alienation from his father
   c. promise to rescue Antigone
   d. resolution to dethrone his father   4. _____

5. What happens in the final scene?
   a. Antigone escapes the vault.
   b. Haimon commits suicide.
   c. Eurydice leaves Thebes.
   d. Creon is removed from the throne and imprisoned. 5. _____

B. Understanding Greek Tragedy. Write the letter of the *best* answer to each question. *(10 points each)*

6. Which of the following statements about the setting and duration of the play is *correct*?
   a. It has three settings: the palace, a battlefield, and a cave.
   b. The entire play takes place in front of Creon's palace.
   c. The action of the play takes place during no more than an hour.
   d. The action of the play covers about three or four days. 6. _____

continued

28 Teaching Resources E • *Adventures in Appreciation*

NAME _____

CLASS _____ DATE _____ SELECTION TEST—CONTINUED

7. In having Creon harshly threaten and accuse a simple sentry (in Scene 1), Sophocles most probably intended to
   a. provide simple comic relief
   b. show Creon as a stern ruler
   c. reveal Creon's corrupt nature
   d. comment on human incompetence   7. _____

8. The play cannot be understood fully if we forget that its subject (in a real sense) is the ruling house of Thebes and the
   a. curse upon it, with sin begetting further sins
   b. hatred of the citizens for their harsh rulers
   c. quarreling gods who support or hate these rulers
   d. bitter wars between Thebes and its neighbors   8. _____

9. To judge from this play, Greek tragedy must be regarded as a(n)
   a. forerunner of the modern mystery novel
   b. official means of teaching respect for Athenian government
   c. way of teaching respect for one's parents
   d. serious poetic art form concerned with religious and ethical problems   9. _____

10. A function of the Greek chorus is to
    a. introduce all of the characters
    b. state public opinion regarding the unfolding events
    c. make clear the outcome of the play
    d. provide amusing and entertaining diversion   10. _____

TEACHER'S NOTES

JULIUS CAESAR, INTRODUCTION AND ACT ONE
William Shakespeare Text Page 535

OBJECTIVES

Act One
The aims of this lesson are for the student:
- To demonstrate recognition of significant details relevant to the plot, events, and main characters of *Julius Caesar*
- To determine the conflicts within *Julius Caesar*
- To analyze characters' thoughts, feelings, and actions within *Julius Caesar*
- To explain Shakespeare's use of metaphor in a selected passage
- To make inferences about specific characters and events in *Julius Caesar*
- To determine the tone of Scene 3 in *Julius Caesar*
- To identify, by using a chart, the characters and the setting of *Julius Caesar*
- To analyze Shakespeare's technique of characterization within speeches as they apply to speaker, subject, and listener
- To interpret the double meanings of puns as cited in Scene 2
- To interpret a selected passage from *Julius Caesar* and relate its importance to the drama
- To complete an audience chart for a persuasive essay topic

INTRODUCING THE SELECTION

Shakespeare has freely based his play on Sir Thomas North's translation of Plutarch's lives of Caesar, Brutus, and Antony. If you refer students to the selection from Plutarch's *Life of Caesar* (page 290), they will find similarities in points of view—Shakespeare and Plutarch present the same psychological portraits of Caesar and particularly of his assassins.

Neither Plutarch nor Shakespeare, of course, was on hand to observe the events about which he wrote. Plutarch relied on historical data, and Shakespeare relied on Plutarch. Students must understand that Shakespeare's contribution to drama was never that of a plot innovator. He picked up his plots from many sources: from English and Roman history; from available literature and popular stories; from stories in the dramatic repertoire of the Italian commedia dell'arte. What Shakespeare contributed to the dramatic arts were magnificent characters and magnificent language.

You might also refer back to *Antigone* and discuss the general structure of that play compared with that of *Julius Caesar*. The Greek plays had an inner structure consisting of five major parts and two minor parts. The five major parts eventually became the five-act structure of the Elizabethan plays. (The five major parts of the Greek plays, which took place between the choric songs, were called *episodios*.) It is probably for this reason that the Shakespearean plays came to have five acts—at least scholars can make a good case for this theory.

In *Julius Caesar* Shakespeare moves the plot to its crisis by centering the action of the first three acts on the formation of the conspiracy and that of the last two acts on its failure.

Shakespeare's language, renowned for its beauty, wit, and earthiness, frequently poses a problem for students. However, many difficulties with archaic words will be cleared up if the students refer to the footnotes. In some instances context will provide clues to words that have changed in meaning. Alert students to some of these words, such as *trophies,* meaning decorations for the statues of Caesar, in Act One, Scene 1, line 66.

To help bridge the gap between modern and Shakespearean language, paraphrase speeches from the play. Assure students that they will find Shakespeare's language less of a problem as they become more familiar with his idioms.

You may find that some students resist reading a drama written in blank verse. Runover lines, inverted sentences, and other complex sentence patterns present problems. Ideally, you should read the entire play aloud, but this would be extremely

continued ☞

time-consuming. Perhaps a better plan to help convince students that they can handle a verse drama would be to read key scenes aloud and reserve the remainder of the play for home reading. You might even suggest that groups of students get together at their homes or in some public room to read the play aloud on their own. At least in the beginning, you should play a role in dramatizing the rhythms of Shakespeare's language.

You might also use one of the recordings of *Julius Caesar.* Films of the entire play or of key scenes—particularly the forum scene—should certainly supplement the reading.

SUMMARY/PRESENTATION

Act One

In Act One, the exposition in the first scene tells us what has happened before the play opens and introduces the conflict. Caesar is returning to Rome in triumph from his wars with Pompey. The city welcomes him as a returning hero, but, in the first step of the rising action, Marullus and Flavius, like a Greek chorus, reveal that there are mixed feelings about Caesar in Rome. In Scene 2, we get the first ominous foreshadowing of disaster when the Soothsayer warns Caesar, "Beware the ides of March." Here we also learn that Caesar is particularly envied by Cassius, the arch conspirator, and that Cassius is attempting to draw Brutus into his plans. We learn further from Casca that Antony has offered Caesar the crown; Casca becomes another candidate for the conspiracy. By Scene 3, the conspiracy is well under way: the final step is the planting of the letters to ensure Brutus' participation.

All of the major characters, with the exception of Octavius, are introduced in this act. Two characters dominate—Brutus and, even more so, Cassius. In his dialogues with Brutus and then with Casca, we learn that Cassius is calculating, cynical, and ruled by emotions. Casca, on the other hand, is blunt and petty. His chief characteristic seems to be contempt for the common people. Brutus—honest, candid, and noble—is the most cautious of the would-be conspirators. He has not yet made up his mind. We know how highly he is esteemed through what others say of him. Antony is only meagerly portrayed; we know he is loyal to Caesar. The character of Caesar is contradictory. He seems pompous, a braggart. Yet he is also courageous and confident when he dismisses the Soothsayer. In addition, he perceptively recognizes Cassius for what he is.

The play provides an excellent study in direct and indirect presentation of character. In Act One, the students must infer the traits of Caesar from what he says, from what others say about him, and from his actions. In Scene 1, we learn about Caesar from the tribunes. In Scene 2, we get Cassius' impressions of Caesar, as well as Caesar's opinions of Cassius. Note that much of our information comes from what the characters say about each other.

One technique of characterization that Shakespeare uses to advantage is that of contrast. Throughout the play, have students note the contrast in the characters of Brutus and Cassius, Casca and Cassius, Antony and Brutus, Antony and Cassius, Portia and Calpurnia, and Antony and Octavius. The class may begin this comparison by observing the two tribunes in Scene 1. One is more talkative than the other. Together they provide a marked contrast to the mob; possibly they represent the views of citizens of a higher class.

Approximately one month elapses from the opening of Act One to its close. Scene 1 takes place on February 15; Scene 2 follows immediately; Scene 3 takes place on March 14.

Be sure students note the natural events in Scene 3 that create an atmosphere of fear and foreboding: the dark night, the thunder and lightning, the rumors of strange supernatural happenings.

READING/CRITICAL THINKING STRATEGIES

Making Inferences About Character

Before students begin reading Act One of *Julius Caesar,* you may want to suggest that Shakespeare was a master of characterization, that even his minor characters have distinct personalities. Remind students that many scholars and critics agree that Shakespeare's genius lies, at least in part, in his understanding of human nature. Tell

continued ☞

students that as they read they should consider the traits of each character that is introduced. What inferences can students make based upon the character's actions and other character's reactions? You may want to have students complete a chart including each character. After students have completed their reading, ask them to discuss their findings. If actions and decisions are the result of character, what do they think the characters may do next?

Character	Traits	Evidence
Flavius	Contempt for common people	lines 1–2

VOCABULARY The following words are defined in the glossary (the number in parentheses indicates the line where the word first appears).

Act One

Scene 1
knave (15)
concave (44)
exalted (57)
servile (72)

Scene 2
countenance (38)
vex (ed) (39)
conception (s) (41)
cogitation (s) (50)
yoke (61)
fawn (75)
aught (85)
chafe (–ing) (101)
buffet (107)
sinew (s) (108)
recount (165)
entreat (166)
wrought (289)
seduce (d) (292)

Scene 3
conjoint (ly) (29)
construe (34)
infuse (d) (69)
prodigious (77)
sufferance (84)
retentive (95)
base (110)
faction (–ious) (119)
redress (118)
bestow (151)

ANSWER KEYS

READING CHECK

Julius Caesar, Act One Text Page 544

A. 1. The triumphant return of Caesar; the feast of Lupercal
2. "Beware the ides of March."
3. Cassius
4. Cassius
5. Caesar refuses it three times; he then swoons and falls down.

B. 1. The commoners are eager to celebrate Caesar's victory over Pompey's sons; Flavius and Marullus disapprove of Caesar's actions.
2. He dismisses the warning.
3. Cassius tells of having to save Caesar from drowning and of Caesar's epileptic fits.
4. Answers may vary. Students should list two of the following events: The earth is shaking, fire is falling from the sky, a man's hand is burned yet remains unharmed, a lion passes Casca in the street without attacking him, burning men walk the streets, and an owl cries at noon.
5. Casca sees the events as ill omens.

STUDY GUIDE

Julius Caesar, Introduction and Act One Text Page 535

1. a. Shakespeare's birthplace
b. Shakespeare's wife
c. The theater built for Shakespeare's acting company
d. Queen of England, from whose name came the term describing this period in English history—the "Elizabethan" era

continued

2. Plays were performed on a stage in a central courtyard, with the audience sitting in galleries or standing in the yard. There was no curtain to mark the change of scenes, and no artificial lighting. There were props and lavish costumes but little scenery as we know it today. Women's roles were played by men.

3. An acting company attached to a particular theater performs several plays in a season, rotating the performances. Members of the company continually rehearse and perform a number of roles.

4. a. Something that is out of place for its time period. Not knowing enough about ancient Rome, for example, Shakespeare introduced into *Julius Caesar* objects that were not yet invented or used.

   b. An "agreement" shared by audience and playwright that a certain dramatic element will have a commonly understood interpretation

   c. A speech by a character spoken alone onstage, used to convey his thoughts to the audience

5. Marullus understands the Second Commoner to mean he is a mender of bad *souls* and thus finds him impudent ("saucy") when he says he can mend Marullus. Likewise, the commoner is having some fun when he says he meddles with no tradesman's or women's matters, but with "awl"—which sounds like *all*.

6. a. He has established himself as a military hero, bringing glory to Rome. He must be a strong, forceful leader.

   b. They see him as authoritarian and power-hungry, about to subvert Rome's republic in order to tighten his control.

   c. He has epilepsy and one deaf ear.

7. First Cassius brags that he openly faced the storm (lines 46–52), contrasting his own boldness with Casca's timidity and fear. Then he suggests that Caesar is like the "dreadful night."

8. a. The conspiracy against Caesar; the fight between Caesar's supporters and opponents

   b. Antony

   c. Cassius, Casca, Cinna, possibly Brutus

9. Cassius is the primary instigator. His strategies include the following behaviors: (a) He uses flattery, calling Brutus noble, good, gentle, worthy. (b) He appeals to Brutus's pride in the republic, referring to another Brutus who would not have stood for a king. (c) He uses deceit, sending fake letters to make it appear there is a groundswell of popular opposition to Caesar.

10. (a) The soothsayer's warning, "Beware the ides of March" (b) The terrible storm, along with the unnatural events described by Casca

11. Sentences will vary.

12. Answers will vary.

13. Responses will vary.

BUILDING VOCABULARY

Julius Caesar, Act One   Text Page 544

Answers may vary slightly, depending on the dictionary used; these are based on *Webster's New World Dictionary, Third College Edition*.

1. A male servant; a man of humble birth or status
2. slavish, submissive, cringing, abject
3. from Middle English, *vexen*, from Middle French *vexer*, meaning "to vex, torment," from Latin *vexare*, meaning "to shake, agitate"
4. (1) To punch; to slap (2) To beat back; to thrust about (3) To struggle against; to force away
5. conjointly
6. grammar
7. three; second
8. (1) A tendon (2) Muscular power or strength (3) Any source of power or strength
9. To speak or write (of)
10. work
11. Having or showing little or no honor, courage, or decency; mean; dishonorable; cowardly; morally low
12. yes

SELECTION VOCABULARY TEST

Julius Caesar, Act One   Text Page 544

A. 1. d   6. b
    2. h   7. e
    3. f   8. c
    4. a   9. j
    5. i   10. g

B. 1. d   4. g
    2. h   5. c
    3. a   6. e

SELECTION TEST

Julius Caesar, Act One   Text Page 544

A. 1. b   6. c
    2. d   7. b
    3. d   8. b
    4. a   9. a
    5. b   10. b

B. 11. b   13. c
    12. c   14. a

Reading Check

NAME _____
CLASS _____ DATE _____ SCORE _____

Julius Caesar *William Shakespeare* (Page 544)

──────────── **READING CHECK** ────────────

Act One

A. Short Answer. In the space provided, write the answer to each question.

1. For what celebrations are the people preparing in the first scene? _____
2. What warning is given to Caesar by the soothsayer? _____
3. Who first speaks to Brutus about the danger of Caesar's growing power? _____
4. Whom does Caesar fear because he "has a lean and hungry look"? _____
5. What happens when Antony offers Caesar a crown? _____

B. 1. In Scene I, why are Flavius and Marullus angry with the commoners?

_____
_____
_____

2. What is Caesar's response to the soothsayer's warning?

_____
_____
_____

3. What two examples does Cassius cite when emphasizing to Brutus Caesar's physical weaknesses?

_____
_____
_____

continued ☞

NAME _____

CLASS _____ DATE _____ READING CHECK—CONTINUED

4. Give two of the unnatural events that alarm Casca.

_____

_____

_____

5. What meaning does Casca attach to these events?

_____

_____

_____

Study Guide

NAME _____

CLASS _____ DATE _____ SCORE _____

INTRODUCTION and JULIUS CAESAR, ACT ONE (Pages 535–563)

William Shakespeare (1564–1616)

Understanding the Writer and His Background

1. Identify each of the following items that relate to Shakespeare's life:

   a. Stratford-on-Avon: _____

   b. Anne Hathaway: _____

   c. The Globe: _____

   d. Elizabeth: _____
   _____

2. Briefly describe the Shakespearean theater.
   _____
   _____
   _____
   _____

3. What is a "repertory system"?
   _____
   _____
   _____

4. Define these terms as they apply to Shakespeare's plays:

   a. anachronism: _____
   _____
   _____

continued

36 Teaching Resources E • *Adventures in Appreciation*

NAME _____

CLASS _____ DATE _____ STUDY GUIDE—CONTINUED

    b. convention: _____
_____

    c. soliloquy: _____
_____

Understanding the Act

Scene 1

5. The humor of the opening lines revolves around puns. Explain the puns on the words "soles" (line 14) and "awl" (lines 21–22).

_____
_____
_____
_____
_____
_____

Scene 2

6. Shakespeare creates a mixed impression of Caesar; as with any human being, Caesar is neither all good nor all bad.

    a. What is there about Caesar that attracts such a strong following? _____
_____

    b. What do his opponents dislike about him? _____
_____
_____

    c. What two physical problems of Caesar's are revealed? _____
_____

continued ☞

Teaching Resources E • *Adventures in Appreciation*

NAME _____

CLASS _____ DATE _____ STUDY GUIDE—CONTINUED

Scene 3

7. How does Cassius use the storm to manipulate Casca?

_____
_____
_____
_____

The Act as a Whole

8. In Act One, Shakespeare introduces the major characters and themes of the play.

   a. What emerges as the central conflict in the play? _____
   _____

   b. Name at least one person who might remain on Caesar's side. _____

   c. Name at least two persons who might oppose Caesar. _____
   _____

9. Who is the main instigator of trouble against Caesar? Explain at least two strategies he uses in his effort to bring Brutus into the conspiracy.

_____
_____
_____
_____
_____
_____

10. There are at least two major hints or omens suggesting right away in the first act that trouble is in store. What are they?

_____
_____
_____

continued ☞

38 Teaching Resources E • *Adventures in Appreciation*

NAME _____

CLASS _____ DATE _____   STUDY GUIDE—CONTINUED

Understanding Vocabulary

11. After checking their meanings in the glossary, use each of the following words in a sentence that pertains to the play.

    a. servile (page 546): _____
    _____

    b. fawn (with the meaning that applies on page 549): _____
    _____

    c. construe (page 557): _____
    _____

    d. prodigious (page 558): _____
    _____

    e. base (with the meaning that applies on page 559): _____
    _____

    f. redress (page 559): _____
    _____

Understanding Literary Elements

12. In this first act, through his techniques of *characterization,* Shakespeare leads us to form certain impressions of the characters. For each character listed below, write at least three adjectives which summarize your own opinion of him at the end of Act One. Then cite two specific things this character said or did that led you to form this opinion.

    a. Cassius: _____
    _____
    _____

    b. Casca: _____
    _____
    _____

continued

NAME _____

CLASS _____ DATE _____   STUDY GUIDE—CONTINUED

   c. Brutus: _____

   _____

   _____

   d. Caesar: _____

   _____

   _____

Writing and Responding to Literature

13. At this point in the play—the end of Act One—have you taken sides for or against Caesar, or are you neutral? Explain your reaction to the growing conspiracy.

Building Vocabulary

NAME _____

CLASS _____ DATE _____ SCORE _____

Julius Caesar, Act One — *William Shakespeare* (Page 544)

USING THE DICTIONARY

A modern desk dictionary does more than give the meanings of a word. It also gives the pronunciation, the word's history (its etymology), its parts of speech, important synonyms and antonyms, related forms of the word, and notes on usage of the word. A guide in the front of the dictionary explains how to interpret the information.

ACTIVITY

Use a desk dictionary recommended by your teacher to answer the following items.

1. What is an archaic (old, now rarely used) meaning for the word *knave*? _____
   _____
   _____
   _____

2. Give three synonyms (words of similar meaning) for the word *servile*. _____
   _____
   _____
   _____

3. Briefly describe the etymology (history) of the word *vex*. _____
   _____
   _____
   _____

4. What does the verb *buffet*, pronounced bŭf′ĭt, mean? _____
   _____
   _____
   _____

continued ☞

NAME _____

CLASS _____ DATE _____ BUILDING VOCABULARY—CONTINUED

5. What is the adverbial form of *conjoint*? _____
_____
_____
_____

6. In what field of study does the word *construe* have a specialized meaning? _____
_____
_____
_____

7. How many syllables are there in the word *prodigious*? Which syllable is stressed? _____
_____
_____
_____

8. How many meanings does the noun *sinew* have? What are they? _____
_____
_____
_____

9. What is an obsolete (no longer used) meaning for the word *entreat*? _____
_____
_____
_____

10. *Wrought* is the alternate past tense and past participle for what word? _____
_____
_____
_____

continued

NAME _____

CLASS _____ DATE _____ BUILDING VOCABULARY—CONTINUED

11. The word *base* has so many meanings that most dictionaries split them into different entries (base^1, base^2, and so on). What meaning of *base* goes with the synonyms *ignoble* and *comtemptible*? _____

_____

_____

_____

12. Is *give* a synonym for *bestow*? _____

Selection Vocabulary Test

NAME _____

CLASS _____ DATE _____ SCORE _____

Julius Caesar, Act One   *William Shakespeare*   *(Page 544)*

---------- **VOCABULARY TEST** ----------

A. Match each word in column I with the correct definition in column II. Place the letter of each definition you choose in the space provided. (7 points each)

I	II
____ 1. knave	**a.** to irritate
____ 2. concave	**b.** slavish; submissive
____ 3. countenance	**c.** a tendon
____ 4. vex	**d.** a male servant
____ 5. conception	**e.** to struggle against
____ 6. servile	**f.** the expression on a person's face
____ 7. buffet	**g.** to win someone over to one's side
____ 8. sinew	**h.** curved inward
____ 9. wrought	**i.** an idea; a thought
____ 10. seduce	**j.** created; performed
	k. eager; willing

B. Below are quotations from *Julius Caesar* in which an italicized synonym has been inserted in place of a word used by Shakespeare. In the space provided, write the letter of the word(s) Shakespeare used, given in the list below. (5 points each)

a. prodigious   **d.** fawn on   **g.** base
b. united   **e.** yoke   **h.** cogitations
c. entreat   **f.** sublime

____ 1. ". . . if you know / That I do *flatter* men and hug them hard, . . ."

____ 2. ". . . this breast of mine hath buried / Thoughts of great value, worthy *meditations*."

____ 3. ". . . yet *enormous* grown / And fearful, as these strange eruptions are."

____ 4. "What rubbish and what offal, when it serves / For the *dishonorable* matter to illuminate . . ."

____ 5. ". . . so with love I might *beg* you, / Be any further moved."

____ 6. ". . . And groaning underneath this age's *bondage*, / Have wished that noble Brutus had his eyes."

Selection Test

NAME _____
CLASS _____ DATE _____ SCORE _____

Julius Caesar, Act One William Shakespeare *(Page 544)*

A. Understanding the Drama. Write the letter of the *best* answer to each question. *(6 points each)*

1. The opening scene with the tribunes Flavius and Marullus is intended mainly to
   a. give us insight into Caesar as a man
   b. reveal the attitudes of various groups toward Caesar
   c. suggest that the play will be a humorous one
   d. furnish insight into the moods of the Roman Senate 1. _____

2. We receive our first insight into Caesar's character in
   a. Caesar's conversation with Casca
   b. Caesar's conversation with a soothsayer
   c. the first remarks of Cassius to Brutus
   d. Caesar's comments to Antony about Cassius 2. _____

3. To judge from the events in Act One, the political mood and behavior of the Roman populace can best be termed
   a. unswervingly patriotic and firm
   b. discontented and angry
   c. cowardly and timid
   d. fickle and changeable 3. _____

4. From his first appearance, Cassius can be described, above all else, as
   a. envious   c. murderous
   b. ambitious   d. patriotic 4. _____

5. When we first see Brutus, he appears to be
   a. envious of Caesar   c. scornful of all politicians
   b. at war with himself   d. timid and elderly 5. _____

6. We learn that the conspirators are anxious to have Brutus as their leader because
   a. he is clearheaded and shrewd
   b. he will make a popular ruler
   c. his reputation will bring respect to their cause
   d. all the conspirators are timid, indecisive people 6. _____

7. From his first appearance, Caesar appears to be all of the following *except*
   a. self-confident   c. well-known
   b. cheerful   d. powerful 7. _____

8. Casca's account of Caesar's refusal of a crown suggests clearly that Caesar
   a. wants no additional honor or worries
   b. really does desire to be king
   c. cares little about the mood of the Roman people
   d. is always afraid of being provoked into one of his fits 8. _____

continued

9. When Cassius first works on Brutus to join the conspirators, he concentrates on Caesar's
   a. physical weaknesses
   b. mental limitations
   c. failures as a general
   d. administrative inexperience

   9. _____

10. All of the business of strange omens and a terrible storm is intended to
    a. amuse and divert Shakespeare's audience
    b. prepare us for violent happenings
    c. indicate the gods' displeasure with Caesar
    d. suggest Caesar's great power

    10. _____

B. Understanding Meaning. Following are four questions, each involving a quotation from Act One. Choose the *best* interpretation of each. *(10 points each)*

11. Cassius says to Brutus,
    "Men at some time are masters of their fates.
    The fault, dear Brutus, is not in our stars
    But in ourselves, that we are underlings."
    By this statement he means that
    a. they both should accept their station in life
    b. it is their own fault that they are subordinate to Caesar
    c. individuals can do nothing to change their destiny
    d. most people are born to be ruled by tyrants

    11. _____

12. Cassius says of Caesar,
    "And when the fit was on him, I did mark
    How he did shake. 'Tis true, this god did shake."
    His tone of voice suggests
    a. sympathy
    b. disbelief
    c. mockery
    d. amusement

    12. _____

13. Antony responds to Caesar's worried comment on Cassius,
    "Fear him not, Caesar. He's not dangerous,
    He is a noble Roman, and well given."
    We know clearly that Antony is
    a. lying to Caesar
    b. revealing a subtle nature
    c. wrong and speaking with unconscious irony
    d. inclined to trust everyone

    13. _____

14. When Casca tells Cassius that he understands the Senate tomorrow will make Caesar king, Cassius responds,
    "I know where I will wear this dagger then.
    Cassius from bondage will deliver Cassius."
    We can infer that he really is saying he will
    a. kill himself
    b. kill Caesar
    c. defy the Senators
    d. denounce Caesar

    14. _____

TEACHER'S NOTES

JULIUS CAESAR, ACT TWO *William Shakespeare* Text Page 564

OBJECTIVES

Act Two
The aims of this lesson are for the student:
- To recognize the relationship of time between Scene 1 and Scene 2
- To point out important details that relate to characters and plot
- To explain and evaluate Shakespeare's methods of characterization as a literary device
- To apply the philosophy of Stoicism to the characters of Brutus and Portia
- To demonstrate an understanding of irony by applying its meaning to selected dialogue
- To describe and analyze the elements of suspense in *Julius Caesar*
- To identify the changes that have taken place within characters and the effect of these changes on the action in the drama
- To cite and list the appearance and use of a selected word within the drama and to determine its varying meanings in context
- To write an essay comparing and contrasting two female characters in *Julius Caesar*

SUMMARY/ PRESENTATION

Act Two
Act Two is a building act. As the act opens, the conspiracy to murder Caesar has not yet been completely laid open to Brutus. He is being worked upon, directly and indirectly, by conversations and by mysterious letters. (You might point out that the use of the mysterious letter is a favorite device of Shakespeare; it might even be regarded as a convention of sixteenth-century drama.) Ultimately, in Scene 1, Brutus makes the crucial decision and allows himself to be convinced that he must be an instrument of Caesar's death. Another important decision reached in Scene 1 is the conspirators' decision to spare Antony's life.

   In Scene 2, Caesar receives warnings of disaster. His wife, Calpurnia, has dreamed that Caesar was being murdered. She also has heard of the alarming portents in Rome. (Remind students that the use of dreams and supernatural signs is another Shakespearean convention.) Caesar is also told that the morning sacrifice has been ominous. But though he wavers for a brief time and considers *not* going to the Senate, he is convinced by Decius to go. Yet we feel that Caesar might still be saved: in Scene 3, we see Artemidorus, who bears a message warning Caesar to stay clear of the conspirators, and in Scene 4 the Soothsayer reappears and tells Portia he will try to speak to Caesar before he enters the Senate. Shakespeare has carefully built up our sense of impending doom and just as carefully has given us cause to think Caesar might yet escape.

   In Act Two, Brutus has become stronger in his stand. He arouses more sympathy than Cassius, who takes his cues from Brutus. Casca is a hypocrite. Caesar, indecisive on the one hand, overconfident on the other, moves closer to his doom. Antony remains a minor figure. The two women stand in strong contrast to each other: Portia is self-disciplined and courageous, while Calpurnia is nervous, weak, and somewhat unstable.

   Act Two begins on the evening of March 14 and continues through the night and into the early morning hours. Supernatural elements in Act Two include the sacrifice and its outcome, Calpurnia's dream, and her recitation of the horrid sights being seen in Rome.

READING/CRITICAL THINKING STRATEGIES

Analyzing Plot
Before students begin reading Act Two of *Julius Caesar,* you might ask them to discuss what conflicts have been established in the play so far. Tell students that as they read, they should pay close attention to the complications and conflicts that appear. You

continued ☞

may need to remind students that some conflicts are internal and that decisions imply conflict. After students have completed their reading, ask them to share their findings and to discuss their reaction to the play to this point. How do they respond to the issues raised?

Conflict/Decision	Response
Brutus decides that Caesar must die for the general good. He has examined his conscience to be sure that he doesn't want Caesar to die for some personal reason.	

ANSWER KEYS

READING CHECK

Julius Caesar, Act Two　　　　Text Page 564

A. 1. Stays awake and debates with himself whether or not Caesar really must be killed
2. All of the conspirators
3. She has had warnings: the troubled heavens, a dream in which she saw Caesar's statue running blood, and interpretations of signs by the augurers, who urge Caesar not to go.
4. Decius Brutus tells him that the Senate is going to offer him a crown and that if he does not go, the Senate will think of him as a coward.
5. To try to warn Caesar on his way to the Capitol

B. 1. He fears that Caesar will abuse his power.
2. Caesar and Antony
3. Brutus will not tell her why he is acting so strangely.
4. It is a warning of the plot to kill Caesar.
5. She dreamed that Caesar's statue ran with blood that came from many wounds and that many Romans smiled and bathed their hands in the blood.

STUDY GUIDE

Julius Caesar, Act Two　　　　Text Page 564

1. Brutus muses on the fact that an ambitious person who seeks and obtains power eventually abuses that power, scorning the very people who helped him achieve it. He speculates that Caesar would likely follow this pattern, thus justifying assassination.

2. a. (a) Calpurnia tells him the watchman has seen terrible, unnatural sights. (b) The augurers found no heart in the sacrificial animal. (c) Calpurnia dreamed that a statue of Caesar spouted blood in which smiling Romans bathed their hands.
   b. (a) His own pride and his disdain for fear or cowardice make him reluctant to stay home. (b) Decius reinterprets Calpurnia's dream in a favorable way. (c) Decius tells him the Senate plans to offer him a crown. (d) Decius suggests he will be mocked if he gives in to Calpurnia's superstitious fears.
3. (a) Artemidorus plans to give him a note revealing the names of the conspirators. (b) The soothsayer plans to remind Caesar of his earlier warning.
4. (a) He is upset and agitated at the thought of the conspiracy. (b) He argues that the conspirators are honest and trustworthy and therefore without need of an oath. (c) He wants to spare Antony, to be "purgers, not murderers." (d) He is loving, respectful, and gentle with his wife. (e) Ligarius reminds us that Brutus is held in unusually high regard and that he need not know where he is going as long as Brutus is leading.
5. a. Brutus considers Caesar in his current political status and can't fault him too severely. But then he imagines Caesar with increased (augmented) power and fears he would abuse it.
   b. A faction is a group of people within an organization working together toward a common purpose, against some other group in the organization. It need not be a conspiracy.
   c. By acting friendly, kind, cheerful, good-natured

continued

48　Teaching Resources E　•　*Adventures in Appreciation*

d. Unpleasantly damp and chilly
e. Omens suggesting the approach of evil: Calpurnia's dream and the unnatural events the guard told her about
f. Ones about to happen

6. (a) The opening of the act shows Brutus still undecided about his course of action. (b) Even after he does decide, Portia tries to dissuade him. (c) At Calpurnia's urging, Caesar wavers about going to the Capitol; Calpurnia and Decius compete in their efforts to influence him. (d) Artemidorus and the soothsayer provide last-minute indications that perhaps Caesar will still be warned in time.

7. Answers will vary, but students should take into account that Brutus is basing his momentous decision on a hypothetical concern—that Caesar *might* abuse power—and not on anything Caesar has actually done.

LANGUAGE SKILLS

Julius Caesar, Acts One and Two   Text Page 544

A. 1. directly, direct
    2. modestly, modest
    3. indifferently, indifferent
    4. carelessly, careless
    5. easily, easy
    6. truly, true
    7. conjointly, conjoint
    8. boldly, bold; wrathfully, wrathful
    9. merrily, merry

B. 10. fully
   11. dully
   12. shrilly
   13. noiselessly
   14. angrily
   15. mightily
   16. guiltily
   17. ordinarily
   18. When adding the suffix –ly to an adjective that ends in –ll, add the letter y only.
   19. When adding the suffix –ly to an adjective that ends in y, change the letter y to the letter i and add –ly.

C. 20. sourly
   21. suspiciously
   22. hastily
   23. patiently
   24. secretly

D. Exact wording may vary.
   25. Brutus listened to Cassius cautiously.
   26. The conspirators quietly talked at Brutus' house.
   27. They unwisely decided not to kill Antony.
   28. Calpurnia urgently begged Caesar to stay home.
   29. Caesar calmly explained Calpurnia's dream to Decius.
   30. Decius persuasively appealed to Caesar's pride.

BUILDING VOCABULARY

Julius Caesar, Act Two   Text Page 564
1. increase
2. aroused
3. affable
4. interposed
5. beg
6. dispersed
7. damp
8. constancy

SELECTION VOCABULARY TEST

Julius Caesar, Act Two   Text Page 564

A. 1. h   6. e
    2. d   7. a
    3. f   8. j
    4. k   9. c
    5. b   10. i

B. 1. e   4. a
    2. h   5. d
    3. c   6. g

Reading Check

NAME _____

CLASS _____ DATE _____ SCORE _____

Julius Caesar *William Shakespeare* (Page 564)

─────────────── **READING CHECK** ───────────────

Act Two

A. Short Answer. In the space provided, write the answer to each question.

1. What does Brutus do on the night before Caesar is murdered? _____

2. Who comes to Brutus' house that night? _____

3. Why is Calpurnia afraid to have Caesar go to the Senate? _____
   _____
   _____
   _____

4. Caesar agrees to stay at home, but then changes his mind. Why does he change his mind?
   _____
   _____
   _____

5. When he meets Portia, where is the soothsayer going? _____
   _____
   _____
   _____

B. 1. Why does Brutus fear Caesar's growing power?
   _____
   _____
   _____

continued ☞

NAME _____

CLASS _____ DATE _____ READING CHECK—CONTINUED

2. What two people does Cassius want to murder?

_____
_____
_____

3. When Brutus returns from his meeting with the conspirators, why is Portia upset?

_____
_____
_____

4. What is the purpose of Artemidorus' letter to Caesar?

_____
_____
_____

5. Describe Calpurnia's dream.

_____
_____
_____
_____

Teaching Resources E • *Adventures in Appreciation*

Study Guide

NAME _____

CLASS _____ DATE _____ SCORE _____

JULIUS CAESAR, ACT TWO *(Pages 564–583)*

William Shakespeare (1564–1616)

Understanding the Act

Scene 1

1. What in Brutus' reasoning ultimately convinces him that Caesar must be killed?

   _____
   _____
   _____
   _____
   _____

Scene 2

2. Caesar is torn between his desire to go to the Capitol and warnings to stay home.

   a. What are the reasons he is given for staying home? _____
   _____
   _____
   _____
   _____

   b. What factors lead him to want to go? _____
   _____
   _____
   _____
   _____

continued

NAME _____

CLASS _____ DATE _____   STUDY GUIDE—CONTINUED

Scene 3

3. What new warnings lie in wait for Caesar as he nears the Capitol?

_____

_____

_____

The Act as a Whole

4. Shakespeare portrays Brutus as "noble" in spite of his decision to become an assassin. List at least three things in this act which help create a favorable impression of Brutus.

_____

_____

_____

_____

_____

_____

_____

Understanding Vocabulary

5. Answer each of the questions below, using the glossary as needed to check the words in italics.

   a. Brutus thinks about Caesar "for the thing he is" and also "what he is, *augmented*"

   (page 565, lines 29–30). Explain what Brutus has in mind here. _____

_____

_____

   b. What is a *faction* (page 566, line 77)? Is it always a conspiracy? _____

_____

_____

continued

Teaching Resources E • *Adventures in Appreciation* 53

NAME _____

CLASS _____ DATE _____ STUDY GUIDE—CONTINUED

   c. How would the conspiracy demonstrate *affability* (page 566, line 82)? _____
_____

   d. What kind of morning is *dank* (page 571, line 263)? _____
_____

   e. What *portents* is Caesar referring to (page 578, line 80)? _____
_____
_____

   f. What kind of evils are *imminent* (page 578, line 81)? _____

Understanding Literary Elements

6. *Suspense* in literature revolves around uncertainty. In writing a historical play, Shakespeare focused on a series of events whose outcome was already known, yet he had to create enough uncertainty to keep the audience interested and wondering. Identify three means by which Shakespeare creates suspense in this act even though the ultimate outcome of the conspiracy is almost surely known by the audience.

_____
_____
_____
_____
_____
_____
_____
_____
_____

continued ☞

NAME _____

CLASS _____ DATE _____ STUDY GUIDE—CONTINUED

Writing and Responding to Literature

7. Brutus' soliloquy at the beginning of Scene 1 exposes the internal conflict he feels, but it ends with his decision to join the conspiracy. Based on the thoughts he reveals here, do you think he has truly justified the need to murder Caesar— or has he simply rationalized it for himself? Does this soliloquy leave you with a positive or negative feeling toward Brutus? Explain your answers.

Language Skills

NAME _____

CLASS _____ DATE _____ SCORE _____

Julius Caesar, Acts One–Two   *William Shakespeare*   *(Page 543)*

―――――――――――― **FORMING ADVERBS** ――――――――――――

Sometimes a writer can add just one word to make an action or a description very precise. As you read the following lines from Act Two, notice that each of the words ending in *-ly* gives a more exact meaning to a verb.

> **Portia.** . . . You've <u>ungently</u>, Brutus,
> Stole from my bed. And yesternight at supper
> You <u>suddenly</u> arose and walked about,
> Musing and sighing, with your arms across,
> And when I asked you what the matter was,
> You stared upon me with ungentle looks.
> I urged you further, then you scratched your head,
> And too <u>impatiently</u> stamped with your foot.   *(Page 571, lines 237–244)*

Ungently, suddenly, and *impatiently* are **adverbs**—words that modify verbs, adjectives, and other adverbs. Like many adverbs, these three answer the question *How?* or *In what manner?* Adverbs ending in *-ly* are usually formed from adjectives: *ungently* from *ungentle, suddenly* from *sudden, impatiently* from *impatient,* and so on.

ACTIVITY A

Underline the *-ly* adverb or adverbs in each of the following quotations. In the space provided, write the adjective from which each adverb is formed.

_____ 1. But what trade art thou? Answer me directly. *(Page 544)*

_____ 2. . . . I your glass/Will modestly discover to yourself/That of yourself which you yet know not of. *(Page 549)*

_____ 3. And I will look on both indifferently. . . . *(Page 549)*

_____ 4. . . . Cassius is/A wretched creature, and must bend his body/If Caesar carelessly but nod on him. *(Page 551)*

_____ 5. There was a Brutus once that would have brooked/The eternal Devil to keep his state in Rome/As easily as a king. *(Page 552)*

_____ 6. And tell me truly what thou think'st of him. *(Page 553)*

continued ☞

56 Teaching Resources E • *Adventures in Appreciation*

NAME _____

CLASS _____ DATE _____   LANGUAGE SKILLS—CONTINUED

_____ 7. When these prodigies/Do so conjointly meet, let not men say/"These are their reasons, they are natural." *(Page 557)*

_____ 8. And, gentle friends,/Let's kill him boldly, but not wrathfully. *(Page 569)*

_____ 9. Good gentlemen, look fresh and merrily. *(Page 570)*

ACTIVITY B

In the blank, write the *-ly* adverb that is derived from each adjective. You may want to check spelling in a dictionary.

10. full _____

11. dull _____

12. shrill _____

13. noiseless _____

14. angry _____

15. mighty _____

16. guilty _____

17. ordinary _____

18. Complete the spelling rule: When adding the suffix *-ly* to an adjective that ends in *ll*, _____

19. Complete the spelling rule: When adding the suffix *-ly* to an adjective that ends in *y*, _____

ACTIVITY C

In the blank, write an *-ly* adverb that could replace the underlined expression.

EXAMPLE   Brutus wandered about <u>in a dreamy way</u>. dreamily

_____ 20. Casca can tell you <u>in his sour fashion</u> what has happened.

_____ 21. Caesar regarded Cassius <u>in a suspicious way</u>.

_____ 22. Cassius moved <u>with haste</u> to build support for his plot.

continued

NAME _____

CLASS _____ DATE _____ LANGUAGE SKILLS—CONTINUED

_____ 23. Portia assured Brutus that she could bear <u>with patience</u> his secrets.

_____ 24. The conspirators met <u>in secret</u> to plot Caesar's death.

ACTIVITY D

Combine each pair of sentences. Change the second sentence into an *-ly* adverb and insert it in the first sentence. Place the adverb near the word it modifies.

    EXAMPLE   Brutus slept. His sleep was not sound.

                       Brutus slept unsoundly.

25. Brutus listened to Cassius. Brutus was cautious.

_____

_____

26. The conspirators talked at Brutus' house. Their voices were quiet.

_____

_____

27. They decided not to kill Antony. This decision was unwise.

_____

_____

28. Calpurnia begged Caesar to stay home. Her speech was urgent.

_____

_____

29. Caesar explained Calpurnia's dream to Decius. Caesar was calm.

_____

_____

30. Decius appealed to Caesar's pride. He was persuasive.

_____

_____

Teaching Resources E • *Adventures in Appreciation*

Building Vocabulary

NAME _____

CLASS _____ DATE _____ SCORE _____

Julius Caesar, Act Two *William Shakespeare* (Page 564)

───────────────── USING SYNONYMS ─────────────────

Synonyms are words that have the same, or almost the same, meaning. Most often, the words are not quite the same in meaning. These shades of difference usually make one synonym more appropriate than another in a given context.

ACTIVITY

After each of the following sentences, a vocabulary word (italicized) and one of its synonyms appear in parentheses. Write in the blank the more appropriate choice for completing the sentence. Use your dictionary as necessary.

1. With sensible exercise, a person's stamina and muscle tone will

   _____.
   (increase/*augment*)

2. The detective's suspicions were _____ when the murder weapon was found in the suspect's car.
   (*instigated*/aroused)

3. The _____ young boss always greeted the employees with a cheery "Good morning."
   (obliging/*affable*)

4. In the middle of the debate, an impatient reporter _____ a question.
   (*interposed*/interfered)

5. After sneezing repeatedly at the dinner table, the polite guest said, "I

   _____ your pardon."
   (*entreat*/beg)

6. At the end of the long, boring lecture, the students _____ quickly.
   (*dispersed*/dispelled)

7. Hours after the swim, the girl's long hair was still _____.
   (damp/*dank*)

8. The young athlete had great _____ in sticking with the training program.
   (*constancy*/stability)

Teaching Resources E • *Adventures in Appreciation* 59

Selection Vocabulary Test

NAME _____

CLASS _____ DATE _____ SCORE _____

Julius Caesar, Act Two *William Shakespeare* (Page 564)

VOCABULARY TEST

A. Match each word in column I with the correct definition in column II. Place the letter of each definition you choose in the space provided. (7 points each)

I	II
____ 1. augment	**a.** to chop or cut
____ 2. instigate	**b.** friendly
____ 3. interim	**c.** to make clean by removing impurities
____ 4. revel	**d.** to urge into action
____ 5. affable	**e.** to introduce an interruption of speech or motion
____ 6. interpose	**f.** the time between one event and another
____ 7. hew	**g.** to foretell the future
____ 8. chide	**h.** to increase; to make greater
____ 9. purge	**i.** unpleasantly damp and chilly
____ 10. dank	**j.** to scold mildly
	k. to engage in lively festivities

B. Below are quotations from *Julius Caesar* in which an italicized word or phrase has been inserted in place of a word used by Shakespeare. In the space provided, write the letter of the word Shakespeare used, given in the list below. (5 points each)

a. prodigies   **d.** constancy   **g.** entrails
b. augur   **e.** phantasma   **h.** visage
c. dismember   **f.** tinctures

____ 1. "... all the interim is / Like a *phantom* or a hideous dream."

____ 2. "Oh, then by day / Where wilt thou find a cavern dark enough / To mask thy monstrous *face*?"

____ 3. "Oh, that we then could come by Caesar's spirit / And not *cut* Caesar!"

____ 4. "It may be these apparent *unusual happenings*, / The unaccustomed terror of this night..."

____ 5. "I have made strong proof of my *steadfastness*, / Giving myself a voluntary wound / Here in the thigh."

____ 6. "Plucking the *organs* of an offering forth, / They could not find a heart within the beast."

TEACHER'S NOTES

JULIUS CAESAR, ACT THREE — William Shakespeare — Text Page 584

OBJECTIVES

Act Three
The aims of this lesson are for the student:
- To select correct details that apply to the plot and characters of *Julius Caesar,* Act Three
- To state opinions and interpretations about characters, actions, and events in Act Three
- To make inferences about characters by evaluating and using information found in dialogue
- To recognize the dramatic structure of Acts One through Five
- To interpret the irony in selected passages
- To take notes for emotional appeals to support an opinion

SUMMARY/ PRESENTATION

Act Three
The turning point or crisis occurs in Act Three, as it does in all of Shakespeare's plays. It occurs at the point at which the hero's fate is in the balance. This situation is similar to the balance of a plane on a fulcrum. The plane could be tilted with ease in one of two directions:

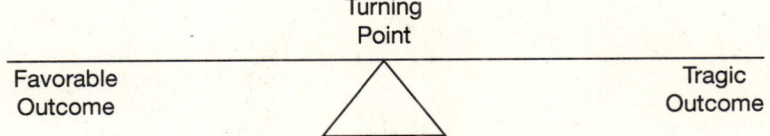

As the act opens, Caesar enters the Senate for the last time. He is surrounded by the conspirators, and at a command from Casca, he is stabbed at least once by each. The cruelest blow of all is dealt by Brutus.

It is with this thrust of the knife that Caesar covers his head with his robes and takes the blows of the other conspirators. Caesar lies dead, and the conspirators are elated. But then Antony seeks permission to speak at Caesar's funeral. Brutus sees no reason to refuse. Cassius, more wily than Brutus, more distrustful, does not think it prudent for Antony to speak, but he gives permission. Antony will give the funeral oration. *The play is approaching its turning point.* One of the most famous pieces of dialogue in all of Western drama is Mark Antony's funeral oration. It is at this moment that the turning point occurs.

Beginning with the lines "Friends, Romans, countrymen . . ." in Scene 2, the scales begin to tip in favor of Caesar's supporters. With his speech, Antony turns the crowd against Cassius and Brutus. This funeral oration is an outstanding example of the power of words. (You might at this point mention that it is said that oratory and military force control the destiny of the world. Mussolini, Hitler, Churchill, and Roosevelt were all masters of oratory.) Scene 3 ends the act with mob action against the conspirators. (You might use this portion of the play to discuss irrational mob violence.)

READING/CRITICAL THINKING STRATEGIES

Evaluating
Before students begin reading Act Three of *Julius Caesar,* suggest that critics disagree about the most important conflict in this play. Some see it as the struggle between good, but flawed, individuals (Brutus vs. Antony). Others see it as a struggle between tyranny and democracy or as a struggle between ambitious men and an easily misled populace. Tell students that as they read this part of the play they should decide what the most crucial issue in the play is. Students might benefit from keeping a chart like the one on page 62. After students have completed their reading, ask them to share their findings and to discuss whether these issues seem relevant today.

continued ☞

Conflict	Issue Raised	Response
Brutus and Cassius discuss Popilius.	Who is to be trusted?	
Caesar tells Metellus not to kneel.	Is Caesar being honest or pretending to be humble?	

ANSWER KEYS

READING CHECK

Julius Caesar, Act Three Text Page 584

A.
1. They petition him to free Metellus' banished brother.
2. Casca
3. To speak at Caesar's public funeral
4. Antony's
5. Because he bears the same name as one of the conspirators

B.
1. Octavius
2. "Et tu, Brute?" (And you too, Brutus?)
3. Answers may vary. Students should give one of the following conditions: Antony may not blame the conspirators for Caesar's death; he must say nothing but good about Caesar; and he must say that he speaks with the conspirators' permission.
4. Caesar left seventy-five drachmas to each man, and his private gardens to the people of Rome.
5. They flee from Rome.

STUDY GUIDE

Julius Caesar, Act Three Text Page 584

1. (a) Artemidorus and the soothsayer both make contact with Caesar, but he fails to take them seriously enough. (b) An ambiguous remark by Popilius suggests that plans for the assassination might have been leaked.
2. a. Caesar again shows the mix of qualities that have made him an honored leader but also the target of assassins. His outburst that he will not be swayed by fawning or flattery seems admirable. His insistence that he is "constant as the Northern Star" reveals his boastful, stubborn side.
   b. Answers will vary.
3. They are easily manipulated, swayed by whatever person captures their attention. First they cheer Brutus, even suggesting that he should be crowned in place of Caesar. They just as quickly turn around and give their allegiance to Antony.
4. He lets himself be overcome with grief at the thought of Caesar's death. He refutes Brutus' claim regarding ambition by mentioning a scene the crowd itself witnessed—Caesar's refusal of the crown three times. He appeals to the crowd's humanity. He arouses gratitude toward Caesar by reading the will. He imagines the dead man's thoughts upon seeing that his friends—especially Brutus—were traitors. All the while, of course, he is really mocking the conspirators while calling them "honorable."
5. We see that Antony has whipped the crowd into a frenzy. The townspeople have become a violent, irrational mob ready to avenge Caesar's death even by taking innocent lives.
6. Expressing misgivings about Antony and rightly predicting that Antony might sway the crowd, Cassius exhorts Brutus not to let Caesar's friend speak at the funeral.
7. Sentences will vary.
8. Literally, Antony follows Brutus' directions to "speak all good you can devise of Caesar"—yet the result of his speech is exactly the opposite of what Brutus wanted. Antony's choice of words is also highly ironic. He repeats lines such as "And Brutus says he was ambitious,/And Brutus is an honorable man" in such a way that he imparts the opposite message.
9. Students' answers will vary but should include evidence from the play.

continued

BUILDING VOCABULARY

Julius Caesar, Act Three   Text Page 584

Answers may vary slightly, according to the dictionary used; these are based on *Webster's New World Dictionary, Third College Edition.*

1. *assail:* (a) comes from Latin, *ad + salire,* (b) meaning "to leap on," (c) to assail someone is to "leap at" him or her in a physical or verbal attack.
2. *prostrate:* (a) comes from Latin, *pro + sternere,* (b) meaning "to stretch out before"; a person who is (c) prostrate is lying face down, or "stretched out, before" someone else, usually in humility. (A person may also be made prostrate, or "stretched out," by an emotional stress such as grief.)
3. *mantle:* (a) comes from Latin, *mantellum* or *mantelum,* (b) meaning "cloak," which (c) closely relates to today's meanings of "cloak or cape" or "any covering that conceals."
4. *appease:* (a) comes from Latin, *a + pax,* (b) meaning "to reach peace"; (c) to *appease* someone is to make peace with him or her by giving in. (*Appease* can also mean "to make peaceful" by soothing fears or satisfying needs.)
5. *carrion:* (a) comes from Latin, *caro,* (b) meaning "flesh"; (c) *carrion* means "decaying flesh," or, by association, "something disgusting or repulsive."

SELECTION TEST

Julius Caesar, Acts Two and Three   Text Page 564

A.
1. c
2. d
3. b
4. d
5. a
6. b
7. a
8. a
9. d
10. b

B.
11. b
12. c
13. f
14. d
15. a

Reading Check

NAME _____
CLASS _____ DATE _____ SCORE _____

Julius Caesar *William Shakespeare* (Page 584)

―――――――― **READING CHECK** ――――――――

Act Three

A. **Short Answer.** In the space provided, write the answer to each question.

1. How do the conspirators manage to gather together around Caesar in the Capitol?
   _____

2. Which of the conspirators makes the first strike with the dagger? _____

3. What favor do the conspirators grant Antony? _____

4. Whose oration succeeds in winning the mob? _____

5. Why does the mob kill Cinna the poet? _____
   _____
   _____

B. 1. Who has Caesar named as his heir?
   _____
   _____

2. What are Caesar's dying words?
   _____
   _____

3. Give one of the conditions under which the conspirators allow Antony to speak at Caesar's funeral.
   _____
   _____
   _____

64 Teaching Resources E • *Adventures in Appreciation* continued ☞

NAME _____

CLASS _____ DATE _____ READING CHECK—CONTINUED

4. What are the contents of Caesar's will?

   _____
   _____
   _____

5. After Antony wins over the crowd, what do Cassius and Brutus do?

   _____
   _____
   _____

Study Guide

NAME _____

CLASS _____ DATE _____ SCORE _____

JULIUS CAESAR, ACT THREE   (Pages 584–606)

William Shakespeare (1564–1616)

Understanding the Act

Scene 1

1. How does Shakespeare continue to hold out hope for Caesar at the beginning of the act?

   _____
   _____
   _____
   _____
   _____
   _____

2. Shakespeare presents the last view of Caesar in this scene.

   a. How does Shakespeare portray Caesar as he is about to die? _____
   _____
   _____
   _____
   _____
   _____
   _____

   b. Where do your own sympathies lie at the moment Caesar is stabbed—with the assassins or their victim? Why? _____
   _____
   _____

66   Teaching Resources E   • *Adventures in Appreciation*   *continued*

NAME _____

CLASS _____ DATE _____ STUDY GUIDE—CONTINUED

Scene 2

3. How would you describe the reactions of the townspeople to the assassination?

_____
_____
_____
_____
_____

4. In his speech, Antony shows himself a master of psychology in the way he plays to the crowd's emotions. What are some of the techniques he uses to gain the crowd's support?

_____
_____
_____
_____
_____
_____
_____
_____
_____
_____

Scene 3

5. How does this scene add to your understanding of the commoners, and the effect Antony's speech had on them?

_____
_____
_____
_____
_____
_____

continued ☞

NAME _____

CLASS _____ DATE _____   STUDY GUIDE—CONTINUED

The Act as a Whole

6. How does Cassius prove himself more shrewdly perceptive than Brutus in this act?

   _____

   _____

   _____

Understanding Vocabulary

7. Use each word below in a sentence of your own, conveying the same meaning the word has in the play. Use the glossary to check your work.

   a. prostrate (page 589, line 125): _____

   _____

   b. appease (page 590, line 179): _____

   _____

   c. legacy (page 599, line 125): _____

   _____

   d. rent (page 600, line 163): _____

   _____

Understanding Literary Elements

8. There is a great deal of *irony* in Antony's funeral speech. Irony occurs when a speaker says one thing but means another, or when someone intends one result and brings about another. Briefly describe the ironic nature of Antony's address to the crowd.

   _____

   _____

   _____

   _____

   _____

continued

NAME _____

CLASS _____ DATE _____ STUDY GUIDE—CONTINUED

Writing and Responding to Literature

9. It is easy for a reader or member of the audience—like the crowd—to be swayed first by the noble, respected Brutus and his fine oratory, then by the passionate Antony. But as readers, we can also be more analytical, evaluating the characters and their motives. Shakespeare has purposely not made the assassination a clear-cut case of right or wrong. Brutus *is* honorable, but he is idealistic and naive and himself had many doubts about the conspiracy. Caesar *is* heroic, but boastful and vain. At this critical stage at the end of Act Three, with civil strife looming, explain which side you tend to support.

_____

_____

_____

_____

_____

_____

_____

_____

_____

_____

_____

_____

Teaching Resources E • *Adventures in Appreciation*

Building Vocabulary

NAME _____

CLASS _____ DATE _____ SCORE _____

Julius Caesar, Act Three *William Shakespeare* (Page 584)

―――――――――――――――――― ANALYZING ETYMOLOGY ――――――――――――――――――

In most dictionaries, the etymology, or history, of a word appears within brackets. The history may be placed after the part-of-speech label or near the end of the entry. A guide in the front of the dictionary explains how to read the etymology. For example, you may see the symbol <, which stands for "derived from."

ACTIVITY

Look up the etymology of each italicized word listed below. On the blanks provided, give (**a**) the language from which the word *originally* comes and (**b**) its meaning in that language. (Do not include the Indo-European base or cross references.) Then (**c**) tell how the original meaning is related to the meaning of the word as it is used today.

1. *assail*

   a. original language _____

   b. meaning of original word _____

   _____

   c. relationship of original meaning to meaning of word today _____

   _____

   _____

2. *prostrate*

   a. original language _____

   b. meaning of original word _____

   _____

   c. relationship of original meaning to meaning of word today _____

   _____

   _____

continued

NAME _____

CLASS _____ DATE _____ BUILDING VOCABULARY—CONTINUED

3. *mantle*

  a. original language _____

  b. meaning of original word _____
  _____

  c. relationship of original meaning to meaning of word today _____
  _____
  _____

4. *appease*

  a. original language _____

  b. meaning of original word _____
  _____

  c. relationship of original meaning to meaning of word today _____
  _____
  _____

5. *carrion*

  a. original language _____

  b. meaning of original word _____
  _____

  c. relationship of original meaning to meaning of word today _____
  _____
  _____

Teaching Resources E • *Adventures in Appreciation*

Selection Test

NAME _____

CLASS _____ DATE _____ SCORE _____

Julius Caesar, Acts Two and Three   William Shakespeare
(Page 564)

A. Understanding the Drama. Write the letter of the *best* answer to each question. *(6 points each)*

1. The main reason Brutus joins the conspirators is that
   a. Caesar has punished or exiled many noble Romans
   b. Caesar has defied the Roman constitution by choosing senators himself
   c. Brutus fears Caesar may be corrupted by too much power
   d. Brutus is jealous of the great reputation Caesar has gained   1. _____

2. Caesar decides definitely to go to the Capitol when
   a. Calpurnia tells him about her dream
   b. the respected Cicero urges him to go
   c. Cassius assures him he will be made emperor
   d. Decius tells him that the Senate will offer him the crown   2. _____

3. That Caesar falls in death at the base of Pompey's statue is ironic because
   a. Pompey had a personal grudge against Caesar
   b. Caesar had come to power by defeating Pompey
   c. Pompey too had been stabbed by conspirators
   d. the act fulfilled a seer's prophecy   3. _____

4. The conspirators bathe their hands in Caesar's blood to
   a. show their hatred for Caesar
   b. fulfill a soothsayer's prophecy
   c. frighten the Roman populace
   d. make their act seem like a religious sacrifice   4. _____

5. When Antony meets the conspirators after the assassination, he alternately grieves for Caesar and pledges allegiance to the conspirators. Why?
   a. His grief is sincere; his pledge of allegiance is insincere.
   b. Both his grief and pledge are sincere—provided that Brutus has a reasonable explanation.
   c. Both are insincere; Antony wants only to avoid suspicion.
   d. His grief is pretended; he will gladly join the conspirators.   5. _____

6. Brutus' allowing Antony to give a second funeral oration was which of the following?
   a. An unavoidable decision
   b. An error of judgment
   c. A test of Antony's loyalty
   d. A deliberate test of the Roman populace's mood   6. _____

7. Antony's speech is powerfully effective because it
   a. plays upon the crowd's emotions   c. is dishonest and sly
   b. sticks to facts   d. is eloquent and formal   7. _____

continued

NAME _____

CLASS _____ DATE _____ SELECTION TEST—CONTINUED

8. Which two words does Antony keep repeating in his oration?
   a. Ambitious and honorable
   c. Benevolent and kind
   b. Roman and freedom-loving
   d. Tyrannical and good

   8. _____

9. What is the basic difference between the two funeral orations?
   a. Brutus offends the Roman mob; Antony wins its approval.
   b. Brutus concentrates on Caesar, Antony on Rome's greatness.
   c. Brutus argues that Caesar was ambitious, Antony that he wasn't.
   d. Brutus is rational, Antony fiery and emotional.

   9. _____

10. The Roman who seems to change the most following Caesar's death is
    a. Brutus
    c. Cassius
    b. Antony
    d. Casca

    10. _____

B. Identifying Characters. Following are five quotations, taken from the first three acts of the play. Using the list of characters below, identify the character *referred to* in each quotation. Use a lettered name only once. (*8 points each*)

   a. Antony   d. Casca
   b. Brutus   e. Cassius
   c. Caesar   f. Cicero

11. "Oh, he sits high in all the people's hearts,
    And that which would appear offense in us
    His countenance, like richest alchemy,
    Will change to virtue and to worthiness."

    11. _____

12.   ". . . dost thou lie so low?
    Are all thy conquests, glories, triumphs, spoils,
    Shrunk to this little measure? Fare thee well."

    12. _____

13. "Oh, let us have him, for his silver hairs
    Will purchase us a good opinion . . ."

    13. _____

14. "What a blunt fellow is this grown to be!
    He was quick mettle when he went to school."

    14. _____

15.   ". . . for he is given
    To sports, to wildness, and much company."

    15. _____

Teaching Resources E • *Adventures in Appreciation*

TEACHER'S NOTES

JULIUS CAESAR, ACT FOUR — *William Shakespeare* Text Page 607

OBJECTIVES

Act Four
The aims of this lesson are for the student:
- To determine the motives of specific characters by using relevant details and events to support responses
- To identify setting and specific events within the fourth act of *Julius Caesar*
- To point out the relationship between selected characters within Act Four
- To determine the symbolic meaning of the ghost of Caesar
- To describe the mood of Scene 3 and to analyze the relevant details of setting and action that contribute to the mood
- To distinguish between and identify metaphor and extended metaphor in selected passages of *Julius Caesar*
- To write an essay explaining the dream images in Acts One through Four and to use specific evidence to support the findings
- To gather supporting evidence for an opinion

SUMMARY/PRESENTATION

Act Four
Act Four begins the falling action. In Scene 1, Antony, Octavius, and Lepidus are in Rome, commenting on their next moves. Who is to be eliminated? How should they tamper with Caesar's will? They, like the conspirators, have axes to grind. In Scene 2, we have the first key incident in the falling action: Cassius and Brutus argue. They and their forces have met at Sardis in Greece, some distance from Rome and some time after Caesar's death. (You might explain to students that time and distance were of little concern to Shakespeare.) Brutus and Cassius now have to contend with the forces of Octavius, Antony, and Lepidus, and their military setbacks affect their personal relationship. In Scene 3, Brutus and Cassius decide to attack the armies of the Triumvirate at Philippi—another unwise decision. Their problem is that their tired army will oppose an army which has been waiting and resting. Having made the decision, Brutus and Cassius part. Brutus goes to his tent to retire, but notice that he is unwilling to be alone. One of his young attendants sings quietly in an attempt to soothe him. To add to his troubles, Brutus has learned that his wife has killed herself. In a sense he is alone now, except for Cassius. When Brutus finally dozes, the ghost of Caesar appears. (Remind students that the use of spirits was another convention in Elizabethan dramas.) Caesar's ghost proclaims that he will meet with Brutus at Philippi.

As the fortunes of the conspirators descend, the stars of Antony and Octavius rise. Have the class comment on the tone at the beginning of Act Four. Is it ominous, sinister, treacherous? Note that Antony and his partners are deciding who, including their own relatives, shall die.

READING/CRITICAL THINKING STRATEGIES

Expressing an Opinion
Before students begin reading Act Four of *Julius Caesar*, discuss their opinions of Brutus, Antony, and Cassius. You may want to list their reactions on the chalkboard. Tell students that as they read they should consider each character carefully. Do their actions serve to confirm or alter their opinions? After students have finished reading, ask them to share their findings. Have their opinions changed or remained the same? Why?

continued ☞

ANSWER KEYS

READING CHECK

A. 1. A triumvirate: Antony, Octavius, and Lepidus
2. Lepidus
3. He does not think Cassius has been behaving honorably; also Cassius refused Brutus the gold he asked for with which to pay his soldiers.
4. She has committed suicide.
5. At Philippi

B. Answers will vary. Students should list the following major events: Antony plans to change Caesar's will, reducing the amount of money given in some bequests, and he reveals his intentions to eliminate Lepidus from the triumvirate; Cassius and Brutus quarrel; Brutus reveals Portia's death and decides that the conspirators' forces will meet those of the triumvirate at Philippi; Brutus sees Caesar's ghost, which tells Brutus he will see him at Philippi.

STUDY GUIDE

1. In Act Three, Antony is impassioned and grieving, devious in his manipulation of the crowd but certainly arousing sympathy. In Act Four he is calmly planning murders, tampering with Caesar's will, questioning whether Lepidus is fit to share power. In short, Antony is demonstrating the very ambition and abuse of power that Brutus feared in Caesar.
2. The Triumvirate is shown in a bad light in Scene 1; in Scene 2 the leaders of the conspiracy are shown to be quarreling. It seems that neither side has reached a very lofty moral ground.
3. a. That Brutus condemned Lucius Pella, failing to honor Cassius' intercession in his behalf
   b. That Cassius took bribes and failed to send him money to pay his army
   c. He tells Cassius that Portia has killed herself.
4. a. That they wait for the enemy forces and thus gain needed rest while their opponents tire themselves out on the march
   b. That they march to the enemy camp at Philippi, thus preventing the enemy from replenishing its forces with neighboring townspeople
   c. Some students might realize that Brutus has not been a wise strategist. His decisions to spare Antony and let him speak were disastrous; one can't help but suspect that this might be another disastrous decision.
5. It suggests Brutus' troubled spirit and also serves as another ominous warning.
6. a. Hidden, secret
   b. Messala's letters give the same news; they're of the same general nature.
7. Antony compares Lepidus to an ass (a beast of burden whose usefulness is over once it has hauled a load) and to a horse (that can be taught menial tasks and then turned to pasture). In other words, Lepidus is good only for following rather simple orders. Brutus accuses Cassius of shallowness in comparing him to a horse; a horse appears spirited before a race but then loses its spark when it feels the spur, that is, when it is pushed onward.
8. Answers will vary.

BUILDING VOCABULARY

1. apparition
2. chastised
3. bay
4. covert
5. salutation
6. tenor

Reading Check

NAME _____

CLASS _____ DATE _____ SCORE _____

Julius Caesar *William Shakespeare* (Page 607)

―――――――――――― **READING CHECK** ――――――――――――

Act Four

A. Short Answer. In the space provided, write the answer to each question.

1. After the conspirators flee, who rules Rome? _____
_____

2. Of the three rulers, which one is not respected by the other two? _____

3. Why is Brutus angry with Cassius? _____
_____
_____

4. What has happened to Portia in the time that Brutus has been away? _____
_____

5. Where does the ghost of Caesar say he will see Brutus again? _____

B. List the major events in Act Four in the order in which they occurred.

_____
_____
_____
_____
_____
_____
_____
_____

76 Teaching Resources E • *Adventures in Appreciation*

Study Guide

NAME _____
CLASS _____ DATE _____ SCORE _____

JULIUS CAESAR, ACT FOUR (Pages 607–623)

William Shakespeare (1564–1616)

Understanding the Act

Scene 1

1. How is the opening of Act Four a sharp and rather unsettling contrast to the close of Act Three?

Scene 2

2. How does Scene 2 parallel Scene 1?

Scene 3

3. In Scene 3, Cassius and Brutus argue.

   a. What is Cassius' complaint against Brutus? _____

continued

NAME _____

CLASS _____ DATE _____ STUDY GUIDE—CONTINUED

   b. What is Brutus' complaint against Cassius? _____

    _____

   c. To what does Brutus attribute his moodiness? _____

    _____

4. Later (page 618), Cassius and Brutus discuss military strategy.

   a. What does Cassius propose? _____

    _____

    _____

   b. What does Brutus propose? _____

    _____

    _____

   c. What is your reaction as Brutus wins the argument? Explain whether you think they make the right decision. _____

    _____

    _____

    _____

5. What is the dramatic effect of the ghost's visit?

_____

_____

_____

Understanding Vocabulary

6. Use the glossary to answer each question below.

   a. What kind of matters are *covert* (page 609)? _____

    _____

continued

78 Teaching Resources E • *Adventures in Appreciation*

NAME _____

CLASS _____ DATE _____ STUDY GUIDE—CONTINUED

b. What does Messala mean when he says he has letters of the same *tenor* (page 617)?

_____

_____

Understanding Literary Elements

7. Shakespeare uses many *metaphors* in his writing. He compares two essentially unlike things to suggest unusual images and associations. More direct comparisons, using the word "like" or "as," are *similes*. Describe the parallel similes in Scenes 1 and 2 by which Antony and Brutus both show scorn for their supposed friends.

_____

_____

_____

_____

_____

_____

_____

_____

Writing and Responding to Literature

8. Explain who you think "wins" the argument between Brutus and Cassius in Scene 3 (pages 611–615). Do you believe Cassius when he suggests he was misrepresented to Brutus by a messenger (page 614, lines 83–84)?

_____

_____

_____

_____

_____

_____

_____

Building Vocabulary

NAME _____

CLASS _____ DATE _____ SCORE _____

Julius Caesar, Act Four   *William Shakespeare*   (Page 607)

─────────────── **USING WORDS IN CONTEXT** ───────────────

ACTIVITY

From the following list, choose the word that best fits in each blank in the paragraphs below. You may need to change slightly the word's form—for example, put a verb in the past tense. (Notice also that you will not use every word in the list.)

covert	chastise	bay	proscription
salutation	legion	tenor	apparition

It would not be surprising if someone driving through the Catskill Mountains of New York were to hear what sounded like rumbles of thunder on a perfectly clear day or see strangely dressed men playing a bowling game, for it is in these mountains that Washington Irving's famous story "Rip Van Winkle" is set. Indeed, it would be only the men's quaint appearance, that of time travelers from a distant century, that would tell you that they were a(n)

(1) _____, not a reality.

By today's standards, Rip Van Winkle did not have much ambition. He did not want to become his time's equivalent of a chief executive officer, nor was he interested in self-improvement through diet or exercise. Instead, Rip was content to fish or to walk through the woods all day. Rip's wife, however, was not happy with this idleness. Known throughout the

village for her sharp tongue, she (2) _____ Rip constantly, making his life miserable. Even Rip's dog, Wolf, was not immune from this scolding. Hunting in the woods,

Wolf could (3) _____ .

Rip's life changed one day when, during a walk in his beloved Catskills, Rip lay down to think

in a (4) _____ part of the woods where he could be alone. As he was about to leave for home, Rip heard his name being shouted. Then he saw a strange old man

whose only (5) _____ was a gesture for Rip to help him with a keg he carried on his shoulder. Although the greeting was somewhat unusual, Rip helped the stranger carry his burden up the mountainside to an open area where a group of these strangely dressed men played the game of ninepins. While they played, the men drank from the liquor in the keg and continued their game. However, when Rip drank repeatedly from the keg, he fell into a deep sleep that lasted twenty years.

When Rip finally awoke and returned to his village, the appearance of the village and the

villagers seemed strange to him. Also, he did not get the (6) _____ of what the village men were saying because he was unacquainted with strange things they were talking about, such as citizens' rights, elections, and Congress. The story has a happy ending, however, for Rip lived out the rest of his life in happy idleness in his now-grown daughter's home.

80   Teaching Resources E   •   *Adventures in Appreciation*

TEACHER'S NOTES

JULIUS CAESAR, ACT FIVE
William Shakespeare Text Page 624

OBJECTIVES
Act Five
The aims of this lesson are for the student:
- To identify specific events and characters important to the plot of *Julius Caesar*
- To evaluate the behavior of the four main characters in *Julius Caesar*
- To make inferences about characters and events in Act Five
- To determine the mood of Scene 1, Act Five
- To identify the function and purpose of a selected scene
- To write an editorial expressing an opinion on a recent coup d'état

SUMMARY/PRESENTATION
Act Five
Act Five presents a long dénouement of war and death. The conspirators die—Cassius and Brutus by suicide. The power is passed to Octavius. Antony's final lines honor Brutus. Referring to the conspirators, he says of Brutus: "This was the noblest Roman of all." Would your students make this claim for Brutus?

READING/CRITICAL THINKING STRATEGIES

Evaluating
Before students begin reading Act Five of *Julius Caesar*, you might ask them to describe the characteristics of a valuable public servant. What differences do they see in their expectations and the expectations of Roman citizens? What were Caesar's characteristics? Tell students that as they read this Act they should consider what is revealed about Brutus, Cassius, Octavius, and Antony in the last scenes. What are the similarities and differences among these characters? Whom do students believe is "the noblest Roman of them all?" Ask students to share their findings about each character and to discuss their choices.

Character	Traits Revealed/Confirmed
Octavius	Points out others' mistakes

ANSWER KEYS

READING CHECK

Julius Caesar, Act Five Text Page 624

A. 1. Antony, Octavius, Brutus, and Cassius
2. No
3. He erroneously believes that his troops, under Titinius, have been beaten.
4. Close to defeat, he runs on his own sword, held by the servant Strato.
5. He calls him "the noblest Roman of them all."

B. 1. Cassius'
2. The eagles that followed his forces from Sardis have been replaced by ravens, crows, and hawks, which fly above them as if in search of prey.

continued

3. Pindarus'
4. Titinius meets friendly troops who give him a victory wreath sent by Brutus to Cassius.

STUDY GUIDE

Julius Caesar, Act Five   Text Page 624

1. As he has done throughout the play, Shakespeare alternates feelings of hope and doom, indications of victory with those of defeat. Right away Octavius expresses glee at the battle situation, but then he argues mildly with Antony—a bad sign. Cassius remarks on an evil omen to which he now gives credence—birds whose shadows seem "a canopy most fatal," and he and Brutus exchange long final farewells; but suddenly in Scene 2, Brutus sees cause for optimism in their military position.
2. He has ordered his forces to attack Octavius' forces too early.
3. Cassius mistakenly believes his friend Titinius to be taken by the enemy. Overcome with grief and a sense that the conspiracy has lost, he tells his servant Pindarus to stab him—with the very sword Cassius himself used against Caesar. We have also learned that this is Cassius' birthday. Titinius returns to find Cassius dead, realizes what has happened, and kills himself with Cassius' sword.
4. They think they have captured Brutus, when actually their prisoner is Lucilius.
5. Brutus—having seen the bodies of Cassius and Titinius, recognizing there is no hope for a military victory, haunted by thoughts of Caesar's ghost—runs on his own sword as Strato holds it for him.
6. They spare Lucilius and others who served Brutus, offering them a place in the new regime. They also accord Brutus all due respect, acknowledging his superior qualities as a human being and planning a proper burial for him.
7. He creates characters who exhibit both positive and negative characteristics. Moreover, just when the audience is likely to favor one side or one character, Shakespeare cleverly tips the scale in the other direction. An obvious example is the shift in Antony from the end of Act Three to the beginning of Act Four. This continual seesawing occurs until the very end. Even Cassius, who appeared so devious and self-serving in Act One, seems more sympathetic at the end, worried about the omen, loyal to Brutus and Titinius. It is hard to cheer his death, just as we certainly cannot cheer Brutus'; yet the final portrait of Antony—the cause of these deaths—is a positive one. Shakespeare permits no final "right" or "wrong."
8. Shakespeare uses the word with two meanings simultaneously. Messala is bemoaning the misunderstanding that resulted in Cassius' death. He refers to the error that is "conceived,"—that is, "understood"; but in the birth imagery, the word also takes on the meaning of "became pregnant."
9. Answers will vary. Most students will probably regard Brutus, and perhaps Caesar, as a tragic hero.
10. Answers will vary.

LANGUAGE SKILLS

Julius Caesar, Acts Three–Five   Text Page 584

A.
1. bleeding
2. mourning
3. well-belovèd
4. cursèd
5. new-planted
6. married
7. tried
8. cooling
9. enforcèd

B. Exact wording may vary.
10. Metellus appeals to Caesar to restore citizenship to his banished brother.
11. The frightened masses demanded an explanation of Caesar's death.
12. The mob stirred with a new-found affection for Caesar.
13. News of Cassius' death will touch Brutus like piercing steel.
14. Antony's soldiers stand behind him with drawn swords.

BUILDING VOCABULARY

Julius Caesar, Act Five   Text Page 624

1. ~~weepy~~; disconsolate
2. ~~make like a snail~~; tarry
3. ~~really arrived at~~; attained
4. ~~rack up~~; engender
5. ~~dreamed up~~; conceived
6. ~~ring of posies or something like that~~; garland
7. ~~powwow~~; parley
8. ~~happening~~; rite

continued

SELECTION VOCABULARY TEST

Julius Caesar, Acts Three–Five   Text Page 584

1. f	3. k	5. l	7. e	9. a
2. b	4. d	6. h	8. g	10. j

SELECTION TEST

Julius Caesar, Acts Four–Five   Text Page 607

A. 1. d 5. b
2. c 6. d
3. a 7. c
4. d 8. a

B. 9. c 13. a
10. b 14. c
11. d 15. b
12. b

Reading Check

NAME _____

CLASS _____ DATE _____ SCORE _____

Julius Caesar *William Shakespeare* (Page 624)

── **READING CHECK** ──

Act Five

A. Short Answer. In the space provided, write the answer to each question.

1. Which generals meet briefly before the Battle of Philippi? _____
_____

2. Should they lose the battle, does Brutus seem willing to be taken back to Rome as a prisoner? _____

3. Why does Cassius have Pindarus kill him? _____
_____

4. How does Brutus die? _____
_____

5. What tribute does Antony pay Brutus? _____
_____

B. 1. Whose birthday is it?
_____
_____
_____

2. What has Cassius seen that, to some extent, makes him believe in omens?
_____
_____
_____

continued

84 Teaching Resources E • *Adventures in Appreciation*

NAME _____

CLASS _____ DATE _____   READING CHECK—CONTINUED

3. Whose mistake leads to Cassius' death?

_____
_____
_____

4. When Titinius goes out to identify the approaching troops, what happens to him?

_____
_____
_____
_____

Study Guide

NAME _____
CLASS _____ DATE _____ SCORE _____

JULIUS CAESAR, ACT FIVE (Pages 624–639)

William Shakespeare (1564–1616)

Understanding the Act

Scenes 1 and 2

1. How does Shakespeare maintain an element of suspense even here in the final act?

Scene 3

2. Brutus has made one more wrong decision. What is it?

3. Describe the circumstances of Cassius' and Titinius' deaths.

continued

86 Teaching Resources E • *Adventures in Appreciation*

NAME _____

CLASS _____ DATE _____   STUDY GUIDE—CONTINUED

Scene 4

4. What mistake do Antony's soldiers make?
   _____

Scene 5

5. Describe the circumstances of Brutus' death.
   _____
   _____
   _____

6. How do Octavius and Antony show compassion (as well as good political sense) at the end?
   _____
   _____
   _____

Understanding the Play As a Whole

7. It is not accidental that readers probably feel ambivalent about both sides in this conflict between the conspirators and Caesar's avengers—perhaps leaning first toward one side, then toward the other. Explain how Shakespeare maintains a sort of balance throughout the play.
   _____
   _____
   _____
   _____
   _____
   _____
   _____

continued

Teaching Resources E • *Adventures in Appreciation*

NAME _____

CLASS _____ DATE _____   STUDY GUIDE—CONTINUED

Understanding Vocabulary

8. Explain the pun on the word "conceived" on page 631, line 69.

_____

_____

_____

_____

_____

Understanding Literary Elements

9. A *tragic hero* is a major character who brings about his downfall through some failure of insight or personality. Explain whether you consider this play to have a tragic hero, or perhaps more than one.

_____

_____

_____

_____

_____

_____

Writing and Responding to Literature

10. Judging from this play alone, what do you foresee as the outcome for Rome? Consider what you know of the characters who will assume power, the "fickle" commoners, and the obvious deep divisions created by Caesar's assassination.

_____

_____

_____

_____

_____

_____

Language Skills

NAME _____
CLASS _____ DATE _____ SCORE _____

Julius Caesar, Acts Three–Five *William Shakespeare* (Page 584)

FORMING ADJECTIVES FROM VERBS

Verbs express action and therefore enliven a piece of writing. Adjectives derived from verbs can also bring a sense of action to the words they modify. Note, for example, the underlined words in the following passage from Act Three of *Julius Caesar*.

> But I am constant as the Northern Star,
> Of whose <u>true-fixed</u> and <u>resting</u> quality
> There is no fellow in the firmament.
> The skies are painted with <u>unnumbered</u> sparks,
> They are all fire, and every one doth shine,
> But there's but one in all doth hold his place. *(Page 586, lines 60–65)*

As you know, adjectives modify, or describe, nouns and pronouns. In the excerpt, *true-fixed* and *resting* modify the noun *quality; unnumbered* modifies the noun *sparks*. These adjectives are derived from verbs. Such verb forms are called **participles**.

The **present participle** of a verb ends in *-ing* (*resting*). The **past participle** of a verb ends in *-ed, -d, -en,* or *-n* (*unnumbered*). Sometimes the participle is combined with another word, often using a hyphen, to form an adjective, as in *true-fixed*. This adjective is a compact way of saying "fixed as true" ("always there"). Participles used as adjectives might be called **verbal adjectives.**

ACTIVITY A

Underline the verbal adjectives contained in the following quotations.

1. Yet see you but our hands/And this the bleeding business they have done. *(Page 590)*

2. Here is a mourning Rome, a dangerous Rome,/No Rome of safety for Octavius yet. *(Page 594)*

3. Through this the well-belovèd Brutus stabbed . . . *(Page 600)*

4. And as he plucked his cursèd steel away,/Mark how the blood of Caesar followed it,/As rushing out of doors, to be resolved/If Brutus so unkindly knocked, or no. *(Page 600)*

5. Moreover, he hath left you all his walks,/His private arbors and new-planted orchards. *(Page 602)*

6. Are you a married man or a bachelor? *(Page 603)*

7. But he's a tried and valiant soldier. *(Page 607)*

8. Thou hast described/A hot friend cooling. *(Page 610)*

9. It useth an enforcèd ceremony. *(Page 610)*

continued

NAME _____

CLASS _____ DATE _____ LANGUAGE SKILLS—CONTINUED

ACTIVITY B

Combine each of the following pairs of sentences. Reduce the second sentence to a verbal adjective and insert it before a noun in the first sentence.

    EXAMPLE   Antony sees the passion of grief. The passion is spreading.

                     Antony sees the spreading passion of grief.

10. Metellus appeals to Caesar to restore citizenship to his brother. Metellus' brother has been banished.

11. The masses demanded an explanation of Caesar's death. They were frightened.

12. The mob stirred with an affection for Caesar. The affection was new-found.

13. News of Cassius' death will touch Brutus like steel. The steel is piercing.

14. Antony's soldiers stand behind him with swords. The swords are drawn.

Building Vocabulary

NAME _____

CLASS _____ DATE _____ SCORE _____

Julius Caesar, Act Five *William Shakespeare* (Page 624)

──────────────── **COLLOQUIAL LANGUAGE** ────────────────

Colloquial words or phrases are expressions appropriate for informal speaking and writing. Such language is not "wrong" but is usually avoided on formal occasions. The vocabulary words you learn in reading literary works can help you improve your own speaking and writing when you want to be more formal, and more exact, in your expression.

ACTIVITY

Each sentence below contains a word or phrase that is too informal for the context. Draw a line through the informal expression. Then write above it the word from the following vocabulary list that best completes the meaning of the sentence. (You may need to change slightly the word's form—for example, put a verb in past tense.)

parley	conceive	rite	engender
disconsolate	tarry	attain	garland

1. In a special address to the nation, the President announced that he was weepy over the resignation of his closest advisor.

2. In a conference with the first-grader's parents, the teacher said, "Your son must make like a snail on the way to school every day, for he's never on time."

3. Spurred on by his ambition, the entertainer has really arrived at a position of being highly regarded in his profession.

4. According to the editorial in the city newspaper, parental involvement in community schools would rack up many positive results.

5. In officially accepting the Nobel Prize, the scientist explained that she dreamed up the new theory after a particular lab experiment gave puzzling results.

6. A champion athlete in the ancient Greek Olympics was honored not with a medal but with a ring of posies or something like that.

continued

NAME _____

CLASS _____ DATE _____ BUILDING VOCABULARY—CONTINUED

7. In a message to the enemy commander, the general suggested that a powwow might avert the necessity of chemical warfare.

8. Every school has a special graduation happening to recognize the accomplishments of those who finish their studies.

Selection Vocabulary Test

NAME _____

CLASS _____ DATE _____ SCORE _____

Julius Caesar, Acts Three–Five   *William Shakespeare*   *(Page 584)*

―――――――――――――― **VOCABULARY TEST** ――――――――――――――

Below are quotations from *Julius Caesar* in which an italicized word or phrase has been inserted in place of a word used by Shakespeare. In the space provided, write the letter of the word Shakespeare used, given in the list below. (10 points each)

- **a.** engendered
- **b.** carrion
- **c.** sublime
- **d.** legacy
- **e.** apparition
- **f.** assailable
- **g.** disconsolate
- **h.** proscriptions
- **i.** revile
- **j.** rites
- **k.** discourse
- **l.** bayed

_____ 1. "... And men are flesh and blood, and apprehensive; / Yet in the number I do know but one / That *vulnerable* holds on his rank."

_____ 2. "... That this foul deed shall smell above the earth / With *decaying* men, groaning for burial."

_____ 3. "... thou shalt *relate* / To young Octavius the state of things."

_____ 4. "... Bequeathing it as a rich *inheritance* / Unto their issue."

_____ 5. "... for we are at the stake. / And *cornered* about with many enemies."

_____ 6. "Mine speak of seventy Senators that died / By their *publication*, Cicero being one."

_____ 7. "I think it is the weakness of mine eyes / That shapes this monstrous *ghost*."

_____ 8. "All *unhappy*, / With Pindarus his bondman, on this hill."

_____ 9. "... Thou never comest unto a happy birth, / But kill'st the mother that *produced* thee!"

_____ 10. "According to his virtue let us use him, / With all respect and *ceremonies* of burial."

Selection Test

NAME _____

CLASS _____ DATE _____ SCORE _____

Julius Caesar, Acts Four and Five   William Shakespeare

(Page 607)

A. Understanding the Drama. Write the letter of the *best* answer to each question. *(9 points each)*

1. The first months of the joint reign of Antony, Lepidus, and young Octavius are marked by
   a. constant battles
   b. a return to democratic rule
   c. squabbles with Roman citizens
   d. bloody purges of notable Romans   1. _____

2. Through their acts and discussions, both sides are shown to have
   a. sincere concern for the welfare of the state
   b. no other desire than for total power and victory
   c. both worthy and unworthy motives and desires
   d. a deep respect for each other and concern for Rome's welfare   2. _____

3. Over Cassius' objections, Brutus decides to do battle at Philippi, his chief argument being that they
   a. are now at their strongest and readiest
   b. will gather many followers as they advance
   c. will seem to be cowards if they remain on the defensive
   d. must capture much food and money, being without either   3. _____

4. In the final two acts of the play, which of the following becomes the chief element of suspense?
   a. Will Caesar be revenged?
   b. Will Brutus and Cassius destroy each other?
   c. Which of the two factions does Rome prefer?
   d. Which rival faction will be victorious?   4. _____

5. A serious mistake that Cassius makes several times is
   a. ignoring the power of the Roman citizenry
   b. permitting Brutus to make bad decisions
   c. undercutting Brutus' actions and decisions
   d. being swayed by omens and soothsayers   5. _____

6. The appearance of Caesar's ghost is an example of
   a. understatement   c. hyperbole
   b. characterization   d. foreshadowing   6. _____

7. Their final conversation before the battle shows Brutus and Cassius as
   a. still unsure of each other
   b. only outwardly reconciled
   c. trusting friends again
   d. fearing each other's treachery   7. _____

continued

94 Teaching Resources E • *Adventures in Appreciation*

NAME_____

CLASS_____ DATE_____ SELECTION TEST—CONTINUED

8. Whether alive or dead, the character who is viewed with the greatest respect by all the other characters is
   a. Brutus
   b. Caesar
   c. Antony
   d. Cassius

   8. _____

B. **Understanding Dramatic Technique.** Write the letter of the *best* answer to each question. *(4 points each)*

9. The arguments, battles, and deaths of the final two acts serve to
   a. suggest that Rome will again be free and happy
   b. indicate that power always destroys itself
   c. make clear the tragic irony in Brutus' motives
   d. destroy the reputation and philosophies of Brutus and Cassius

   9. _____

10. Shakespeare fills the play with omens and predictions. What do they basically provide?
    a. Comic relief mainly
    b. Predictions that come true
    c. Moments of quiet between periods of violence
    d. Sources of alarm to all concerned

    10. _____

11. Shakespeare gives the play a number of conflicts. Which of the following is only a minor conflict?
    a. Brutus' struggle with himself to justify a murder
    b. Conflicts between Brutus and Cassius over strategy
    c. The conflict between Caesar and dissatisfied citizens
    d. A struggle among Caesar's successors for domination

    11. _____

12. Shakespeare is particularly interested in
    a. providing lively spectacle
    b. portraying character
    c. teaching us Roman history
    d. presenting violent action onstage

    12. _____

13. Shakespeare uses foreshadowing in all of the following instances *except*
    a. Cassius' account of Caesar's swimming the Tiber
    b. a terrible storm and unnatural events in Rome
    c. a soothsayer's attempted warning to Caesar
    d. the visit of Caesar's ghost to Brutus' tent

    13. _____

14. The turning point of the play clearly is which of the following?
    a. Brutus' decision to join the conspirators
    b. Caesar's assassination
    c. The reception of Antony's funeral oration
    d. The defeat in battle of Brutus and Cassius

    14. _____

15. Which of the following can be identified as one of the main concerns or themes of the play?
    a. The evil of rebelling against one's ruler
    b. The complexity of right and wrong actions
    c. The danger of following one's impulses
    d. The horror of war

    15. _____

Teaching Resources E • *Adventures in Appreciation*

TEACHER'S NOTES

I NEVER SANG FOR MY FATHER   *Robert Anderson*   Text Page 640

OBJECTIVES

Act One

The aims of this lesson are for the student:
- To demonstrate recognition of the characters, setting, and time frame of events in *I Never Sang for My Father* by using a chart
- To identify the motivations of characters in Act I
- To identify the major conflict presented in first-person point of view
- To evaluate the actions of central characters and to demonstrate the ability to draw inferences from these actions
- To use stage directions to determine the attitude of characters in Act One
- To express opinions and probable outcomes concerning specific characters and events in Act One
- To analyze advertisements for logical fallacies

Act Two

The aims of this lesson are for the student:
- To cite specific details relevant to events and characters in Act Two
- To evaluate the reactions of two characters by contrast and comparison
- To locate specific dialogue within Act Two to support the central theme of the play
- To identify the point of climax in Act Two
- To cite the explanation of the title of the play within the dialogue and to demonstrate the ability to make inferences about the title of the play
- To recognize the significance of a selected statement made by a main character
- To use an outline to organize a persuasive essay

The Play as a Whole

The aims of this lesson are for the student:
- To draw conclusions and demonstrate the ability to make inferences about the central theme of *I Never Sang for My Father*
- To state in one's own words the meaning of selected dialogue of a central character
- To express an opinion about the conclusion of the play
- To define in one's own words the central theme of *I Never Sang for My Father* and to apply this theme to modern life
- To recite specific dialogue in the play and to convey the feelings intended by the author

SUMMARY/ INTRODUCTION

This is a very fine modern drama; in teaching it, be careful not to allow students to view Tom Garrison, the father, as a villain. Some of the subtleties of the play might be grasped more quickly by an adult audience, which is better able to look back and evaluate sibling, maternal, and paternal relationships. All of these relationships are to be found in this play, but the emphasis is on the father/son relationship.

The plot of this play is quite simple. An elderly couple, Tom and Margaret Garrison, have come north from a winter in Florida. This well-to-do couple has the means to maintain homes in Florida and New York's Westchester County. Both husband and wife are in their late seventies and in poor health. They need the attention of their son, Gene, a college professor. Gene is "spiritually" in conflict. About a year before the play opens, his wife died; now he is contemplating remarriage, a decision that will take him to the West Coast. One of the problems in the play is that Gene does not feel free to go. The other major problem is revealed in Gene's opening speech to the audience: he wants to love his father.

continued

The dialogue among the three characters quickly establishes the son's difficulties, with his father in particular. Gene is a gentle, easygoing man, but resentment has developed because the father still tends to see him as a "child," someone to be dominated. (Some of your students will immediately empathize with the son. They will feel sorry for him because he is not able to "live his own life." But be sure to discuss this: Who among us is really free from responsibility?) Father, son, and mother, like all of us, reveal weaknesses and strengths. We learn that Tom had a brutal, poverty-stricken childhood. He was deserted by his own father and forced to support a brother, a sister, and a mother, whom he adored and who died young. We learn further that Tom Garrison is a self-made man. He would consider himself a "man's man": He is proud that his son was a Marine and fond of the company of his cronies. He and Gene actually have strong feelings of affection for each other, but each time a bridge is delicately built, it seems to be torn down. At the end of Act One, Margaret Garrison dies.

In Act Two, Alice, the daughter whom Tom had once banished for marrying someone he disapproved of, is introduced. Students might find it hard to like Alice, who is somewhat abrasive and who disguises her feelings with a hard-boiled exterior. In fact, she is much like her father, while Gene is like his mother. Alice now wants to arrange for Tom's care by someone outside the family, but Gene does not want to destroy the old man's last shred of dignity and independence. Harsh words are said; Alice accuses Gene of being soft and of refusing to face the sadness in life. But Gene decides to ask his father to come with him to live in California, the most loving gesture Gene has made to his father in his life. Tom says no, and not too pleasantly. He cannot let Gene establish his own life (Gene is his "dividend"). Gene's move to California is, to Tom, like another desertion—his father leaving him all over again. Tom sends his son away. Gene comes back once or twice to visit. When Tom visits Gene, Tom becomes ill and is forced to stay in California after all. Tom Garrison dies unable to speak or move. He leaves his son wondering what lies behind the misted-over eyes. The son still does not know, and neither does the audience.

Pay particular attention to the worth of Tom Garrison. Tom Garrison is not a villain—he is a man whose fears make it difficult for him to drop his defenses and show his love for his family. In fact, Tom has the same insecurities that his own son has. He had the same feeling for his mother that Gene has for Margaret. He has, unconsciously, made Gene feel isolated from him in the way he was isolated from his own father.

This play is a slice of reality, open on both ends. It presents an opportunity to discuss the absence of a resolution. The play is a product of the artistry of a modern dramatist. He had it within his power to do what he wanted with the plot. Why did he decide to end the play this way? Do students think this ending, sad as it is, is true to life? Does it help them understand how difficult it sometimes is to "give in" or to correct flaws in ourselves? Does it make them see how difficult it sometimes is to know another person?

READING/CRITICAL THINKING STRATEGIES

Finding Cause-and-Effect Relationships
As a prereading strategy for Act One of *I Never Sang for My Father*, you might assign the parts of the Porter and Gene to students and have them read through Gene's first long speech. Tell students that as they read this part of the play they should consider Gene's relationship with both of his parents. What characteristics does the mother have that make it possible for Gene to love her? What characteristics does the father have that make it difficult for Gene to love him? What characteristics does the father have that make loving him possible? After students have completed their reading, ask them to compare their findings and to discuss their reactions to each of the three main characters.

continued

Father's Character Traits	Evidence	Does Gene Value This Trait? (Explain Your Answer)
refuses to ask for help	scene at train station	

Mother's Character Traits	Evidence	Does Gene Value This Trait? (Explain Your Answer)

Drawing Conclusions

Before students begin reading Act Two of *I Never Sang for My Father,* you might ask them to discuss what people should do when their own emotional well-being conflicts with their duties and obligations to others. Tell students that as they read this part of the play they should consider how each of the characters would answer that question. What clues or evidence can students cite to support their conclusions? After students have finished their reading, ask them to discuss their findings. How do they think Robert Anderson would answer the question?

Clues to Gene's Answer	Interpretation or Implication
says that his mother was terribly concerned about his father's health	seems to indicate that his mother's worry contributed to her death

Clues to Alice's Answer	Interpretation or Implication

Clues to Tom's Answer	Interpretation or Implication

continued

VOCABULARY

The following words are defined in the glossary:

Act One		Act Two			
exasperation	(643)	contort (s)	(664)	tolerable	(677)
nondescript	(646)	sedative	(664)	callous (ness)	(677)
dowager (s)	(646)	elocution	(666)	bereave (d)	(678)
enunciate	(647)	eulogy	(670)	emaciate (d)	(678)
mollify (–ied)	(647)	perpetual	(671)	wrack (ed)	(680)
solicitude	(647)	reflective	(672)	susceptible	(682)
morbid	(650)	appall (s)	(672)	conceive (–able)	(682)
pique (d)	(652)	mystic (al)	(672)	senile (–ity)	(684)
chaise longue	(653)	executor	(672)		
dote (s)	(654)	belligerent	(673)		
incongruous	(656)	cow (ed)	(675)		
cardiogram	(660)	rationalize (–ization)	(677)		

VOCABULARY ACTIVITY

Present to your class the following list of vocabulary words from *I Never Sang for My Father* and the ten sentences that begin after the list. Have students identify the word from the list that fits in the blank in each sentence. Then, have students define each word as it is used in the sentence.

You can present the list and the sentences by writing them on the chalkboard or on a transparency and having students give answers orally or write them on their own paper. Or, you can distribute copies of the list and the sentences and have students write their answers on the copies. If you decide to use copies, be sure to leave sufficient space between sentences for students to write their answers.

bereaved
tolerable
contorts
nondescript
susceptible
cowed
perpetual
enunciate
reflective
belligerent
dotes
piqued
appalls
mollified
chaise longue

1. Angry and _____, the two men faced each other with their hands clenched into fists.

2. Aunt Betty's out back, lying on the _____ under the elm tree, reading a novel.

3. My dog may appear _____ to others, but to me he's special.

4. No, the universe is not _____; scientists believe that it will eventually collapse.

5. His rude behavior _____ me so much that I prefer not to go anywhere in public with him.

continued ☞

Teaching Resources E • *Adventures in Appreciation*

6. People who have light hair and fair skin are particularly _____ to sunburn.

7. Jonathan always enjoys visiting his grandmother, who _____ on him and always buys him little presents.

8. In the summer the subtropical heat was barely _____, even at night.

9. His explanation and sincere apology finally _____ her anger.

10. No one can understand what you're saying when you don't _____ clearly.

Answers

1. belligerent
2. chaise longue
3. nondescript
4. perpetual
5. appalls
6. susceptible
7. dotes
8. tolerable
9. mollified
10. enunciate

ANSWER KEYS

READING CHECK A

I Never Sang for My Father, Act One Text Page 642

A.
1. He wanted to love his father.
2. He wants to marry Peggy and move to California.
3. He says that if Gene moves to California, it will kill his mother.
4. A hard one. His father deserted his family and left them living in a miserable tenement.
5. She dies.

B.
1. In Florida
2. She died a year earlier.
3. Watching television Westerns
4. Margaret is not in good health; she has had two operations for cancer, has arthritis, and, most importantly, has a heart condition which has already led to three heart attacks.
5. Answers will vary. Most students will respond negatively to Tom: He is argumentative, as the opening scene with the bags reveals; his efforts to control his son's life are illustrated by his discouraging Gene from moving to California; he appears to neglect his wife when he decides he wants to have dinner with the Rotary Club rather than sit with her at the hospital.

READING CHECK B

I Never Sang for My Father, Act Two Text Page 664

A.
1. His father talks about himself and not about Margaret.
2. She wants to arrange for someone to come in and care for him.
3. He becomes angry and says he can take care of himself.
4. He asks Gene to bring Peggy back East to live with *him*. He refuses to go to California.
5. They fail. Tom dies alone, and Gene never gets close to him.

B.
1. Answers may vary. Students should list the following events: Gene marries Peggy. When Tom comes for a visit, he is ill, and Gene puts him in the hospital, where he dies.
2. The central conflict is Gene's and Tom's inability to love, understand, and accept each other.
3. At the end of the play, Gene still feels that his father never loved him.

continued

STUDY GUIDE A

I Never Sang for My Father,
Act One Text Page 642

1. a. (1) He doesn't want to pay for a doctor in Florida. (2) He keeps having the diamond ring appraised. (3) He reads the prices on the menu to decide what to order. (4) He explains the amount of tip he leaves.
   b. (1) They vacation in Florida every winter. (2) Margaret wears a mink coat.
   c. (1) He keeps mentioning his association with the Senator, a presumably important person. (2) He seems to go out of his way to get attention—from Mary the waitress, from the nurse, from the Rotarians. (3) He dwells on the past, always reminding people how he rose against tremendous odds.
   d. (1) He was mayor. (2) Margaret in all sincerity calls him remarkable; Marvin Scott says he is "quite a fella."
   e. (1) He is forgetful (hasn't remembered that Gene will be at the station, is confused about the suitcases). (2) He needs a hearing aid. (3) He has a persistent cough.

2. He is clearly left with deep emotional scars inflicted in early childhood. His drunken father left the family in poverty; then his mother died when he was ten years old. This easily accounts for his preoccupation with money, his need for attention, and his failures with his own children.

3. Tom's interests and values reflect his lower-class background. In contrast to her husband—who spends his time watching westerns—Margaret wants to talk about art, music, or books. She is the cultured one and also has more insight. For example, she recognizes that Gene has a future in California and discusses the matter with great sensitivity, also revealing that she has picked out an old-lady's home so as not to be a burden in her old age. Tom, however, becomes highly emotional about the California issue; greatly dependent on his son but unable to admit it, he says it is Margaret who could not tolerate Gene's absence.

4. Answers will vary. It probably indicates his inability to express emotion, his need to hide behind a mask of assumed gaiety.

5. It is strained and confused—still struggling toward some kind of resolution, as Gene says at the beginning. He tries hard to please his father—indeed, to love him—but harbors considerable resentment and can't manage to break through the elaborate shield Tom has built up over the years.

6. a. 2
   b. 1
   c. 4
   d. 2
   e. 4

7. They are more an extension of the play than is usually the case, probably providing more information to a reader than could be conveyed to a member of an audience in a live performance. Many become almost a narration (for example, Gene's thoughts about the quotation on page 655 and about Tom's reminiscences at the end of page 656); others *are* the speaker's silent thoughts ("Here is the subject," on page 653). A direction like that on page 653—"Gene is made uncomfortable . . . but he doesn't show it"—suggests that Anderson does not expect his actors to convey every nuance but to incorporate into their overall performance the thoughts and motivations he supplies.

8. Answers will vary. Most students will probably emphasize Margaret's obvious irritation with her husband, his flirtations, his different interests. Some might focus on her concern for his health and the admiration she holds for him in spite of his frailties.

STUDY GUIDE B

I Never Sang for My Father,
Act Two Text Page 664

1. From early childhood he had been forced to earn money—selling newspapers, dancing in saloons, working at a lumber mill. After taking a night course to learn secretarial skills, he worked his way up in a company from stenographer to vice president. Despising his own father, he didn't want children of his own until Margaret persuaded him after many years of marriage.

2. Dr. Mayberry says immediately that Tom should not be staying there alone, raising the issue of where Tom will live and who will provide care for him. Since this comes from a doctor and from one who has known the family for years, there is no reason to question his judgment. Thus, we know that Gene and Alice are correct when they argue with Tom about this question later.

3. Gene, like Margaret, is the sensitive one. He tries to consider his father's feelings in spite of the deep resentment he harbors. Even at this stage, he longs for a closer, more honest relationship with Tom and is ready to bend over backwards in an effort to achieve it. Alice is like Tom: blunt, unsentimental, confident. She

continued

feels they each must live their own lives and not make undue personal sacrifices for a difficult, irascible father.

4. a. (1) He dwells on the prices of various caskets and even asks whether there is a tax. (2) At the funeral he fumes because he paid $300 for a plot and it is not being maintained well enough. (3) The letter he writes mentions his rise from $5 a week to $50,000 a year.
   b. He says, "I have long gotten the impression that my only function in this family is to supply the money to—." And later, "I was tolerated around this house because I paid the bills and—."

5. Gene loved his mother and shared her interests (especially music); however, he realized he was a welcome but inappropriate substitute for his father. "A son is not supposed to make his mother's life."

6. He has fended for himself since he was a young child and refuses to recognize that he needs help now. Accepting help would be admitting weakness—something he cannot do.

7. a. His mouth is twisted, distorted—as if he is fighting to control his emotions.
   b. He must carry out the provisions of Margaret's will.
   c. He might show hostility or quarrelsomeness by raising his voice, using an angry tone of voice, or gesturing.
   d. He thinks she has become hardened toward their father, that she is unfeeling and insensitive.
   e. Tom has lost an excessive amount of weight, making him look too thin and bony.

8. a. Answers will vary.
   b. Answers will vary.

LANGUAGE SKILLS

I Never Sang for My Father,
Acts One and Two   Text Page 642

A. 1. can't, not
    2. Not many, don't
    3. you'd never, you never
    4. nothing, wasn't
    5. isn't, not

B. 6.–10. Sentences will vary.

C. Exact wording may vary.
   11. The idea scarcely seems to faze her.
   12. We just didn't know any better.
   13. I hardly know those people any more.

14. My business dealings aren't that complex any longer.
    or
    My business dealings are no longer that complex.
15. I don't need anyone to help me.

BUILDING VOCABULARY A

I Never Sang for My Father,
Act One   Text Page 642

Choices of antonyms will vary.
1. correct
2. descriptive, stunning, (an) excellent, etc.
3. correct
4. angered, irritated, enraged, etc.
5. unconcern, indifference, negligence, etc.
6. cheerful, pleasant, etc.
7. correct
8. correct
9. correct
10. harmonious, balanced, etc.

BUILDING VOCABULARY B

I Never Sang for My Father,
Act Two   Text Page 664

1. contortion
2. reflective
3. mystical
4. senility
5. tolerable
6. callousness
7. bereavement
8. conceivable

SELECTION VOCABULARY TEST

I Never Sang for My Father,
Acts One and Two   Text Page 642

A. 1. c   6. k
    2. e   7. a
    3. h   8. g
    4. b   9. j
    5. d   10. f

B. 1. b   4. b
    2. a   5. c
    3. d

continued

SELECTION TEST

**I Never Sang for My Father,
Acts One and Two** Text Page 642

- A. 1. c
- 2. a
- 3. b
- 4. b
- 5. c
- 6. b
- 7. c
- 8. c
- 9. a
- 10. b

- B. 11. b
- 12. a
- 13. c
- 14. a
- 15. c

Reading Check A

NAME _____
CLASS _____ DATE _____ SCORE _____

I Never Sang for My Father   *Robert Anderson*   (Page 642)

READING CHECK

Act One

A. Short Answer. In the space provided, write the answer to each question.

1. At the opening of the play, Gene tells us he loved his mother. What does he tell us about his father? _____

2. What important decision about his own life does Gene discuss with his parents? _____

3. How does his father react to Gene's news about California? _____

4. What kind of childhood did Tom have? _____

5. What happens to Gene's mother at the end of the act? _____

B. 1. Where do Gene's parents spend their winters? _____

2. What happened to Gene's first wife? _____

3. What is Tom's favorite evening pastime? _____

continued

104   Teaching Resources E   •   *Adventures in Appreciation*

NAME _____

CLASS _____ DATE _____ READING CHECK A—CONTINUED

4. Why is Tom worried about his wife?

_____

_____

5. What is your attitude toward Tom—do you like him or dislike him? Give three of his actions or remarks as reasons for your attitude.

_____

_____

_____

_____

_____

_____

Teaching Resources E • *Adventures in Appreciation*

Reading Check B

NAME _____
CLASS _____ DATE _____ SCORE _____

I Never Sang for My Father   *Robert Anderson*   (Page 664)

──────────────── **READING CHECK** ────────────────

Act Two

A. Short Answer. In the space provided, write the answer to each question.

1. Why is Gene annoyed at the way his father acts after Margaret dies? _____
   _____
   _____

2. What does Alice want to do about their father? _____
   _____

3. How does Tom react to Alice's suggestion? _____
   _____

4. What is Tom's response when Gene invites him to live in California? _____
   _____
   _____

5. What happens to Gene's efforts to make peace with his father? _____
   _____

B. 1. Give the major events which occur after Gene moves to California.

   _____
   _____
   _____
   _____

continued ☞

NAME _____

CLASS _____ DATE _____ READING CHECK B—CONTINUED

2. What is the central conflict in the play? _____
_____
_____

3. How might the conflict be viewed as unresolved?
_____
_____
_____
_____
_____

I NEVER SANG FOR MY FATHER, ACT ONE (Pages 640–663)

Robert Anderson (1917–   )

Understanding the Act

1. Tom is a complex character who elicits a variety of contradictory reactions. Give specific examples from the play to show the following points:

   a. He is greatly concerned about money. _____

   b. He doesn't really have to worry about money. _____

   c. He is insecure; he needs to feel important. _____

   d. He has achieved respect and some prominence. _____

   e. He has experienced physical deterioration. _____

continued

NAME _____

CLASS _____ DATE _____ STUDY GUIDE A—CONTINUED

2. What probably accounts for much of Tom's personality, including his difficulty in establishing a close relationship with his son?

_____
_____
_____
_____
_____

3. Briefly contrast the personalities and interests of Tom and Margaret.

_____
_____
_____
_____
_____
_____
_____
_____

4. How do you account for Tom's inappropriate behavior—for example, his remark about Bert Edwards' deceased wife ("Where'd he lose her?"), or his dinner with the Rotarians while his wife lies in the hospital?

_____
_____
_____
_____

continued

Teaching Resources E • *Adventures in Appreciation*

NAME _____

CLASS _____ DATE _____ STUDY GUIDE A—CONTINUED

5. Briefly describe Gene's relationship with his father.

_____
_____
_____
_____
_____
_____
_____
_____
_____

Understanding Vocabulary

6. Write the number for the answer that best matches the meaning of the word in italics.

a. _____ The houses had a certain *nondescript* elegance (page 646).

(1) no longer in fashion   (2) unable to be classified   (3) unpleasant   (4) odd; unusual

b. _____ Tom is *mollified* by the smile (page 647).

(1) soothed   (2) amused   (3) pleased   (4) surprised

c. _____ "Well, I appreciate your *solicitude*" (page 647).

(1) advice   (2) help   (3) support   (4) concern

d. _____ Children see their parents as *forbearing* (page 652).

(1) uninteresting   (2) patient   (3) influential   (4) unimportant

e. _____ Tom's revelation seemed so *incongruous* (page 656).

(1) emotional   (2) sudden   (3) insincere   (4) out of place

NAME _____

CLASS _____ DATE _____ STUDY GUIDE A—CONTINUED

Understanding Literary Elements

7. There is minimal *staging* in this play. The introduction notes the lack of scenery and the reliance on lighting. However, Anderson has included an unusual number of *stage directions,* instructions to the actors written into the script. How are they different from those in other plays you have read?

_____

_____

_____

_____

_____

_____

_____

_____

_____

Writing and Responding to Literature

8. Explain what kind of marriage you think Tom and Margaret had. For example, were they basically happy with each other? Was Margaret understanding enough to accept Tom's irritating habits gracefully? Did Tom's feelings for Helen Moffett influence his marriage? Provide evidence from the play to back up your opinion.

_____

_____

_____

_____

_____

_____

_____

Teaching Resources E • *Adventures in Appreciation*

Study Guide B

NAME _____

CLASS _____ DATE _____ SCORE _____

I NEVER SANG FOR MY FATHER, ACT TWO   *(Pages 664–686)*

Robert Anderson (1917–   )

Understanding the Act

1. What additional details do we learn about Tom's background in this act?

   _____
   _____
   _____
   _____

2. What central issue of this act does Dr. Mayberry raise right away? Why is his remark important?

   _____
   _____
   _____
   _____
   _____
   _____

3. Briefly contrast the personalities and outlooks of Gene and Alice.

   _____
   _____
   _____
   _____
   _____

continued

NAME _____

CLASS _____ DATE _____   STUDY GUIDE B—CONTINUED

4. Even more clearly than Act One, Act Two demonstrates Tom's total preoccupation with money.

   a. Find at least three places where his concern with dollars and cents is totally inappropriate, although highly revealing. _____
   _____
   _____
   _____
   _____
   _____

   b. How is money intimately tied up with Tom's perception of his role in the family?
   _____
   _____
   _____
   _____

5. Considering what you learn in this act, describe Gene's feelings toward Margaret.
   _____
   _____
   _____
   _____

6. Why is Tom so utterly opposed to a housekeeper?
   _____
   _____
   _____
   _____

continued

Teaching Resources E • *Adventures in Appreciation* 113

NAME _____

CLASS _____ DATE _____ STUDY GUIDE B—CONTINUED

Understanding Vocabulary

7. Check the meaning of the italicized words in the glossary to answer each question:

   a. How does Tom look with his mouth *contorted* (page 664)? _____
   _____

   b. What is Tom's role as *executor* (page 672)? _____
   _____

   c. How would Tom show he is *belligerent* (page 673)? _____
   _____

   d. What *callousness* is Gene accusing Alice of (page 677)? _____
   _____

   e. Why is Gene troubled by Tom's *emaciated* body (page 678)? _____
   _____

Writing and Responding to Literature

8. There is little real action in this play, and little attention to setting. The focus is on characterization as, with mixed fascination and horror, we watch this family crisis unfold. Examine your own reactions to these characters as you answer the questions below:

   a. Alice might be hard-hearted in her approach to Tom, but she is realistic and, in many ways, she is right. Gene might be admirable in his desire to remain with his father, but he is perhaps overly self-sacrificing and naive to think things can change. In the long, emotional discussion between Gene and Alice, explain which one you think showed better judgment.

   _____
   _____
   _____
   _____
   _____
   _____

continued

114 Teaching Resources E • *Adventures in Appreciation*

NAME _____

CLASS _____ DATE _____ STUDY GUIDE B—CONTINUED

b. Tom is stubborn, domineering, exasperating; he does invite rejection. Yet his rise from poverty to a position of respect and financial comfort is undoubtedly remarkable, and we do see that he is suffering underneath his mask of invulnerability. What is your overriding feeling toward Tom? Dislike? Pity? Anger? Frustration? Explain whether he elicits your sympathy.

_____

_____

_____

_____

_____

_____

_____

_____

_____

| Language Skills | NAME _____ |
| | CLASS _____ DATE _____ SCORE _____ |

I Never Sang for My Father   *Robert Anderson*   (Page 642)

──────────── **NEGATIVE WORDS** ────────────

English provides various ways to express the **lack of something** or **an opposite quality.** A writer must carefully choose a method of expression to be sure the desired meaning is clear. Notice the different uses of negative words in these two sentences from Act One of *I Never Sang for My Father.*

> Parkview Meadows Estates . . . only there was no meadow, and no park, and no view except of the neon signs of the chain stores. Some old houses remained, like slightly frowzy dowagers. The lawns were not well kept, and the houses were not painted as often as they should have been, but they remained. *(Page 646)*

The playwright uses negative words with the nouns in the first sentence. By doing so, he emphasizes the scene's emptiness, the total lack of something. In the third sentence, the negative *not* modifies an adverb, *well,* and a verb, *were painted.* The use of the negative establishes a contrast between what could be and what is. The homes have the opposite quality of what they could have.

ACTIVITY A

Each of the quotations below is followed by a rephrasing that shifts the negative emphasis of the sentence. Notice how the shift also changes the playwright's meaning. Underline the negative element in each of the following pairs of sentences.

> EXAMPLE   Don't worry about anything now, Dad.   *(Page 643)*
> Worry about nothing now, Dad.

1. But I can't tell you what it's been like.   *(Page 644)*
   But I can tell you what it's not been like.

2. Not many boys have fathers they could be as proud of.   *(Page 652)*
   Many boys don't have fathers they could be as proud of.

3. I know when Carol died, you said you'd never marry again.   *(Page 653)*
   When Carol died, you never said you'd marry again.

4. I was a kid with nothing.   *(Page 656)*
   I wasn't a kid with anything.

5. You're looking for something that isn't there, Gene.   *(Page 678)*
   You're not looking for something that is there, Gene.

continued ☞

116   Teaching Resources E   •   *Adventures in Appreciation*

NAME _____

CLASS _____ DATE _____   LANGUAGE SKILLS—CONTINUED

Using Negatives in Clauses to Show Contrast

Writers frequently show contrast by joining ideas in independent clauses, one containing a negative word.

    EXAMPLE   Death ends a life, <u>but</u> it does <u>not</u> end a relationship. . . . *(Page 642)*

ACTIVITY B

Complete each of the following sentences by adding a clause that contains a negative word.

    EXAMPLE   Tom watched cowboy movies, but <u>he liked **nothing** better than telling someone his life story.</u>

6. Tom asked Gene to stay the night, but _____
_____

7. Gene wanted to share the experience of his mother's death with Tom, but _____
_____

8. Gene thought many people would come to Margaret's funeral, but _____
_____

9. Gene wanted to move to California, but _____
_____

10. Gene thought he was becoming closer to his father, but _____
_____

Avoiding Double Negatives

In formal English, the use of two negative words where one is enough is considered inappropriate.

    EXAMPLE   INCORRECT: I do<u>n't</u> see <u>none</u> of them.

                    CORRECT: I see none of them.

                    CORRECT: I don't see any of them. *(Page 643)*

continued

NAME _____

CLASS _____ DATE _____ LANGUAGE SKILLS—CONTINUED

Negative words that sometimes present difficulty are *none, nothing, no, hardly, barely* and *scarcely*. Remember that with these words, you do not need another negative form in the clause or sentence.

    EXAMPLE We <u>scarcely</u> had time to finish.

                   He felt <u>no</u> sympathy for her.

ACTIVITY C

Rewrite each of the following sentences to eliminate the double negative.

11. The idea doesn't scarcely seem to faze her.

_____

_____

12. We just didn't know no better.

_____

_____

13. I don't hardly know those people any more.

_____

_____

14. My business dealings aren't that complex no longer.

_____

_____

15. I don't need no one to help me.

_____

_____

Building Vocabulary A

NAME _____

CLASS _____ DATE _____ SCORE _____

I Never Sang for My Father, Act One   Robert Anderson   (Page 642)

ANALYZING CONTEXT / IDENTIFYING ANTONYMS

ACTIVITY

Antonyms are words that have opposite meanings. In each of the following sentences, the italicized vocabulary word may be used incorrectly because an antonym of the word is needed. If the vocabulary word is used correctly, leave the sentence alone. If it is used incorrectly, write an appropriate antonym in the blank before the sentence.

_____ 1. The baseball fans showed their *exasperation* with the losing team by jeering loudly.

_____ 2. The building, a *nondescript* example of Greco-Roman architecture, has attracted visitors from all over the world.

_____ 3. Because of the speaker's failure to *enunciate,* most of the audience did not understand the speech.

_____ 4. The ambassador's words so *mollified* several of the member nations at the U.N. that their representatives walked out.

_____ 5. *Solicitude* is an important factor in the cause of many traffic and industrial accidents.

_____ 6. The flight attendant suggested that the passenger, rather than read the article on recent airplane accidents, concentrate on more *morbid* thoughts.

_____ 7. The idea that an inexperienced actor might win the award so *piqued* the older actor that he withdrew from the competition.

_____ 8. One unrealistic aspect of television comedy shows is the portrayal of parents who always *forbear* their children's misbehavior.

_____ 9. The parents so *doted* on the new baby that they would not leave her with a babysitter even on their anniversary.

_____ 10. Much of the restful atmosphere in the newly decorated room came from the careful, *incongruous* blending of colors.

Building Vocabulary B

I Never Sang for My Father, Act Two — Robert Anderson (Page 664)

USING SUFFIXES

A **suffix** is a letter or group of letters added to the end of a word or root to create a new word. The suffix may signal a particular part of speech and thus help you decide how an unfamiliar word is being used in a sentence. Here are some common suffixes that form adjectives and nouns.

Adjective-Forming Suffix	Meaning	Example
-able	able to, capable of	variable
-al	of, like	comical
-ive	having the nature of	derisive

Noun-Forming Suffix	Meaning	Example
-ion	act or condition of	exasperation
-ity	state of	equality
-ment	act or process of	movement
-ness	state or quality of	casualness

ACTIVITY

Each sentence below is followed by a word in parentheses. Choosing from the lists of suffixes above, add the appropriate suffix to the word and write the new word in the blank to complete the meaning of the sentence. Use a dictionary to check the spelling of your answers.

1. In a _____ of pain and grief, the man bent forward and turned his face away when he heard the terrible news. (*contort*)

2. After a _____ moment, my aunt gave us her carefully considered opinion. (*reflect*)

3. Although fortune tellers claim to have _____ powers, most people believe that they are simply good at reading personalities. (*mystic*)

4. Because the elderly woman sometimes could not remember the names of old friends, she feared the onset of _____. (*senile*)

5. Since the invention of air conditioning, life in a hot climate has become more _____. (*tolerate*)

6. Drivers who lock small children or animals in cars on hot days reveal a _____ toward living creatures. (*callous*)

continued

NAME _____

CLASS _____ DATE _____ BUILDING VOCABULARY B—CONTINUED

7. In Western cultures, widows once showed their _____ by wearing dark, somber clothes for a least one year. (*bereave*)

8. In 1960, with the nomination of John F. Kennedy by the Democrats, it became _____ that the United States would elect its first Catholic President. (*conceive*)

Selection Vocabulary Test

NAME _____

CLASS _____ DATE _____ SCORE _____

I Never Sang for My Father   *Robert Anderson*   (Page 642)

---------- **VOCABULARY TEST** ----------

A. Match each word in column I with the correct definition in column II. Place the letter of each definition you choose in the space provided. (5 points each)

I	II
_____ 1. exasperation	**a.** medication that calms and relieves
_____ 2. nondescript	**b.** to pronounce words clearly
_____ 3. dowager	**c.** extreme annoyance
_____ 4. enunciate	**d.** to soothe
_____ 5. mollify	**e.** not having any distinguishing qualities
_____ 6. contort	**f.** lasting forever; eternal
_____ 7. sedative	**g.** the art of speaking in public
_____ 8. elocution	**h.** a well-to-do, elderly woman
_____ 9. eulogy	**i.** to open carefully
_____ 10. perpetual	**j.** a speech delivered at a funeral
	k. to twist into an unusual shape

B. In the space provided, write the letter of the word or phrase closest in meaning to the italicized word. (10 points each)

_____ 1. The baby sitter *cowed* the children into obeying her.
  (a) bribed (b) scared (c) praised (d) tricked

_____ 2. The stranger had a(n) *mystic* air about him.
  (a) mysterious (b) intelligent (c) evil (d) friendly

_____ 3. His actions toward his old friend were *callous*.
  (a) generous (b) expected (c) rude (d) unfeeling

_____ 4. After his friend's accident, Bill's attitude was *morbid*.
  (a) helpful (b) gloomy (c) vengeful (d) concerned

_____ 5. The nurse expressed *solicitude* for the patient's condition.
  (a) encouragement (b) agony (c) concern (d) grief

Selection Test

I Never Sang for My Father   Robert Anderson   (Page 642)

A. Reading Comprehension.   Write the letter of the *best* answer to each question. *(6 points each)*

1. Which of the following statements about the play is *not* correct?
    a. The *time* of the play is about 1965.
    b. The *setting* of the play is the Greater New York area.
    c. The *duration* of the play is about a week.
    d. The play involves several kinds of *conflict*.

2. Tom Garrison is best described as a(n)
    a. frail, elderly man who is becoming senile
    b. unsuccessful businessman
    c. man who loved his father
    d. kind and generous father

3. Margaret Garrison can be described as a(n)
    a. successful businesswoman   c. bad wife
    b. charming, outgoing person   d. impatient woman

4. The play's title is useful chiefly because of its
    a. expression of homesickness
    b. clue as to a major theme of the play
    c. identification of the chief character
    d. foreshadowing of a major discovery in the play

5. In the play's opening scene we learn that
    a. Gene is inconsiderate and thoughtless
    b. Gene's mother is robust and healthy
    c. Gene's father is stubborn and absent-minded
    d. everyone is considerate of everyone else

6. The opening scene performs the following function:
    a. It foreshadows Alice's arrival.
    b. It makes clear the several conflicts between the characters.
    c. It introduces all of the characters.
    d. It reveals Carol's death.

7. Tom's physical and mental condition is made clear in several ways. Which of the following in *not* one of them?
    a. His admitting his mind "is like a sieve"
    b. His mishandling of the suitcases
    c. His difficulty in understanding obvious remarks
    d. His habit of repeating his own stories

8. The character who is most torn with indecision and whose problems are foremost in the play is
    a. Tom   c. Gene
    b. Margaret   d. Alice

continued

Teaching Resources E • Adventures in Appreciation

NAME _____

CLASS _____ DATE _____ SELECTION TEST—CONTINUED

9. The character who has the *least* self-insight is
   a. Tom
   b. Margaret
   c. Gene
   d. Alice   9. _____

10. Margaret's death leaves Gene feeling
    a. deeply guilty
    b. grieving and troubled
    c. secretly relieved
    d. wiser and calmer   10. _____

B. Understanding Drama. Write the letter of the *best* answer to each question. *(8 points each)*

11. As a stage play, this drama is somewhat unconventional in that it
    a. presents action largely through the "eyes" of the two characters
    b. uses the stage very freely to facilitate scene shifts
    c. utilizes one of the characters as a contrast to another
    d. makes use of lighting   11. _____

12. Which of the following best indicates the mood or pace of the play?
    a. Somber and deliberate
    b. Lively and swift
    c. Alternately cheerless and cheerful
    d. Unclear and hesitant   12. _____

13. In what way is a change of scene made in the play?
    a. The curtain goes down briefly.
    b. A turntable stage is rotated.
    c. Lights dim and characters shift stage position.
    d. There are no changes of scene.   13. _____

14. The central dilemma of the play involves
    a. the inability of two people to show love for each other
    b. the problems of old age and illness
    c. the rivalry between parents and children
    d. inability to adjust to the death of a loved one   14. _____

15. The turning point in the play comes with
    a. Margaret's unexpected death
    b. the quarrel between Gene and Alice
    c. Tom's refusing to live with Gene
    d. Gene's moving to California   15. _____

TEACHER'S NOTES

THE THIRD MAN *Graham Greene and Carol Reed*   Text Page 689

OBJECTIVES

The aims of this lesson are for the student:
- To employ a chart for reference on filmmaking terms used in the screenplay *The Third Man*
- To demonstrate recognition of the cast of characters in *The Third Man* and the actors and actresses who portrayed them in the film
- To identify specific details that pertain to characters and events in *The Third Man*
- To draw conclusions about the title of the screenplay and to identify the character to whom the title refers
- To determine the relationship of the subplot to the main plot in *The Third Man*
- To analyze the character of Holly Martins and to cite specific examples within *The Third Man* that reveal his character
- To contrast the characters of Martins and Calloway
- To identify and explain through one method of characterization the character of Harry Lime
- To explain the different effects of setting as they relate to the plot and the characters of *The Third Man*
- To recognize the overall theme of *The Third Man* and its effects on the central characters in the screenplay
- To write an essay comparing Holly Martins' characteristics as an antihero with those of a traditional hero

SUMMARY/ INTRODUCTION

The drama opens with Holly Martins' arrival in Vienna. He has come to work for his old friend Harry Lime and is shocked to learn that Harry has been run over by a car and killed. He is even more shocked—and incredulous—when told by police that Harry was the worst racketeer in Vienna. Students this age relate well to the concepts of loyalty and friendship, and they will understand Martins' reluctance to believe that Harry was not the person he seemed to be.

Martins, along with Harry's girlfriend, Anna, suspect that Harry was murdered and decide to investigate. All who witnessed the accident, except the porter at Harry's flat, maintain that only two men carried Harry's body from the street. The porter insists there were three. After the porter is apparently murdered, Martins' and Anna's suspicions are confirmed. There really was a third man.

Soon afterwards, Martins realizes his own life is in danger when he has to escape pursuit by running to police headquarters. There, he is finally convinced that Harry was involved in a scheme to steal and sell watered-down penicillin. Martins also learns he is being sought for the porter's death. He agrees to leave Vienna.

Having fallen in love with Anna, Martins decides to see her one more time before leaving. Someone in the shadows looks up from the street at Anna's window while Martins is there. After leaving Anna, who has told him she will always love Harry, Martins recognizes Harry standing in a darkened doorway across the street. He gives chase, but Harry eludes him. Martins reports what he has seen to the police who order Harry's coffin to be opened. They discover the body of a missing medical orderly who had implicated Harry in the penicillin scheme.

Martins finally meets Harry face to face and realizes that his friend is really an evil man. Martins agrees to help the police capture Harry in exchange for Anna's freedom from deportation. Anna refuses Martins' offer and turns her back on him.

At last the trap is set, but Anna warns Harry, who then flees. Following a chase through the sewers of Vienna, Martins shoots and kills Harry. On his way to the airport, Martins sees Anna and tries to get her attention, but she walks right past him.

The movie was shot in Vienna in 1949, and students will need to understand the historic relevance of post-World War II Austria to the story. Much of the action takes place in war-torn areas of the city. Anna's difficulty with her papers and Harry's sarcastic comparison of his actions with those of the government both allude to the war and have a major bearing on fully understanding the plot.

continued

Since most students will never have seen a movie being made, they will enjoy the camera action and scene settings in this film play. To help them follow the action, you should review and make certain they understand the film-making terms listed under **Elements of Screenplays**.

Holly Martins, the antihero of the drama, is a character students will like. They will not immediately view him as a failure in life as most adults would. For students to better understand his character, you may want to encourage them to watch for clues that tell them something about Martins' career as a writer. They will receive their first clue at the very beginning from the voice-over that points out that Martins is broke when he arrives in Vienna.

READING/CRITICAL THINKING STRATEGIES

Drawing Conclusions

As a prereading strategy for *The Third Man*, refer students to the discussion of *foreshadowing* in the **Literary Terms and Techniques** section. You may want to remind students that after we have finished reading, foreshadowing may seem obvious, but while we are reading we often miss the foreshadowing or clues that provide us with hints of things to come. Students might discuss how clear or obvious foreshadowing should be. In a mystery, should the foreshadowing actually reveal the ending? Tell students that as they read this drama they should play close attention to any hints that all may not be as it seems. After students have finished their reading, ask them to compare their findings. How would they evaluate the amount of foreshadowing in this drama?

VOCABULARY

The following words are defined in footnotes or in the glossary:

apprehension	(690)	tousled	(701)	ensuing	(709)
subaltern	(694)	tirade	(704)	queue	(714)
undertones	(695)	hideous	(706)	kiosk	(721)
intention	(697)	rigmarole	(706)	protocol	(723)
packet	(699)	unperturbed	(709)	commiseration	(727)

VOCABULARY ACTIVITY

Provide students with the following list of vocabulary words from *The Third Man*.

apprehension
intention
tirade
unperturbed
kiosk
subaltern
packet
hideous
ensuing
protocol
undertones
tousled
rigmarole
queue
commiseration

Ask students to choose five words from the list and to complete some or all of the following exercises for each word.

First, tell students to define each word, giving more information than is found in footnotes or in the glossary in the textbook. Suggest to students that they consult at least two dictionaries or other reference sources to gain an understanding of each word before attempting to define it.

continued

Next, have students give five words or phrases that identify what the word is. For example, the word *smattering* (line 22 in the voice-over at the beginning of the script) is identified with a small number, a taste of something, a shallow understanding, a vague notion, and a bit.

Then, ask students to list five words or phrases that identify what the word is not. For example, a *smattering* is not a lot, many, a large number, in-depth knowledge, or an overabundance.

Finally, have students write an original sentence for each of the vocabulary words. You can review students' responses in class discussion or as a written assignment (either graded or ungraded).

ANSWER KEYS

READING CHECK

A.
1. Harry said that he had work for Holly in Vienna.
2. Diluted penicillin
3. He is a writer.
4. She is Harry Lime's girlfriend.
5. Harbin

B. Answers may vary. Suggested responses appear below.
1. Holly Martins is a naively loyal man who is determined to discover what happened to his friend, Harry Lime.
2. Vienna, Austria, soon after World War II
3. Martins notices discrepancies in the various accounts of Lime's death and wants to find out the truth.
4. Martins, cooperating with the police, finds and kills Lime.

STUDY GUIDE

1. The frequent changes of scene would be difficult to stage. Scenes such as Martins's escape from the cultural center and the chase in the sewer, as well as the background of bombed Vienna, are more easily captured on film.
2. There are just too many "coincidences." It becomes hard to believe that Harry Lime was killed while with two friends, by his own driver, and with his own doctor happening to walk by just afterward.
3. Through Martins' persistent probing, Harry Lime's accomplices realized that the porter had seen the aftermath of the "accident" and that his details conflicted with their own, especially in the matter of how many people were carrying the body.
4. The third man must have been Harry Lime himself, helping to carry the dead man, who was actually Harbin. The men killed Harbin because he had informed on them, and now they staged Harry's death to help him escape the law.
5. a. It provides the right climate in which a man like Harry can operate. It also gives him a pretext for his actions: "In these days, old man, nobody thinks in terms of human beings. Governments don't so why should we?"
   b. The fragmentation of the city works to Harry's advantage; he knows he is safe as long as he stays in the Russian zone. The situation of the zones also arises in the issue of Anna's forged papers.
6. a. Answers will vary, although students should recognize that he was a charmer who made people laugh and feel good.
   b. Holly Martins and Anna both look back upon him as someone who "could fix anything": to avoid an exam, to get papers forged. Perhaps his trickery with cards at age fourteen was innocent enough, but that instinct coupled with his charm helped him manipulate people and situations for corrupt purposes.
   c. Answers will vary.
7. Sentences will vary.
8. a. Students will note that he is devoted to his friend and determined to uncover what he perceives as a murder. Yet some of the steps he takes can be seen as foolhardy as well as admirable. He is obviously a second-rate writer although a popular one, is broke upon arrival in Vienna, and seems rootless.
   b. Answers will vary.
9. Answers will vary, although some students might feel it had something to do with Anna, since he was near her house.

continued ☞

LANGUAGE SKILLS

A. 1. advances to meet him, holds out an envelope—verbs or predicates
2. tousled hair, hopeless eyes—noun phrases
3. opens the drawer, pulls out a comb—verbs or predicates
4. drops the comb, slams the drawer to, puts her hand over her face—verbs or predicates
5. watching the scene, waiting his opportunity—participles or participial phrases

B. Exact wording may vary.
6. Martins vowed to avenge his friend Harry and rescue Anna from the police.
7. Martins seeks out the porter, who witnessed the accident, and Dr. Winkel, who attended Harry at the accident scene.
8. Harry hides in the sewers, and there he shoots Paine.
9. Calloway wasn't interested in whether Harry Lime was killed by his friends or by accident.
10. Calloway said that Harry was a racketeer and a child murderer.

C. Words repeated for emphasis are italicized below. Answers may vary slightly.
11. hanging *on the* walls, perched *on the* cupboards
12. *I've been* frightened, *I've been* alone, *I've been* without friends and money, *I've* never known anything like this
13. sometimes hurrying *too much*, then slowing *too much*
14. *Stealing* penicillin from the military hospital, *diluting it to* make it go further, *selling it to* patients
15. *I saw him* buried, *I've seen him* alive

D. 16.–20. Answers will vary.

BUILDING VOCABULARY

1. a
2. a
3. b
4. a
5. b
6. b
7. b
8. a

SELECTION VOCABULARY TEST

A. 1. e
2. f
3. h
4. a
5. j
6. b
7. i
8. g
9. d
10. c

B. 1. c
2. a
3. d
4. a

SELECTION TEST

1. c
2. d
3. b
4. b
5. a
6. c
7. c
8. d
9. b
10. a

Reading Check

NAME _____

CLASS _____ DATE _____ SCORE _____

The Third Man *Graham Greene* and *Carol Reed* (Page 687)

---------- **READING CHECK** ----------

A. Short Answer. In the space provided, write the answer to each question.

1. Why does Holly Martins come to see Harry Lime? _____
_____

2. What did Harry Lime sell on the black market? _____
_____

3. What is Holly Martins' occupation? _____
_____

4. Who is Anna Schmidt? _____

5. Who is buried in Lime's coffin? _____
_____

B. 1. Identify the major character in the story and write one sentence describing that character.

_____
_____

2. What is the setting of this story? _____
_____

3. What is the central conflict or problem facing the main character or characters?
_____
_____

4. How is the conflict or problem resolved at the end of the story?
_____
_____

Study Guide

NAME _____

CLASS _____ DATE _____ SCORE _____

THE THIRD MAN (Pages 687–739)

Graham Greene (1904–   ) and Carol Reed (1906–1976)

Understanding the Drama

1. *The Third Man* was originally a novel and was then made into a screenplay. How does it seem more suitable for film than for live theater?

   _____
   _____
   _____
   _____

2. Why does Holly Martins suspect that Harry Lime was murdered, not accidentally killed?

   _____
   _____
   _____
   _____

3. Why was the porter killed?

   _____
   _____
   _____
   _____

4. Who was the third man that the porter saw? Describe what really happened.

   _____
   _____
   _____
   _____

continued

NAME _____

CLASS _____ DATE _____ STUDY GUIDE—CONTINUED

5. The opening of the drama immediately establishes the setting—a war-torn city with its Black Market and its confusion of occupiers speaking different languages and presiding over different zones.

   a. How does the Black Market atmosphere influence the plot and characters? _____
   _____
   _____
   _____

   b. How does the existence of the zones facilitate the action of the drama? _____
   _____
   _____
   _____

6. We don't see much of Harry, but what we do see does not appear very admirable.

   a. Does it seem reasonable to you that Harry attracted people like Holly and Anna?
   _____
   _____
   _____

   b. Where do we learn that racketeering would not, after all, be alien to Harry's nature?
   _____
   _____
   _____
   _____

   c. Do you sympathize with Harry when he is killed? Why or why not? _____
   _____
   _____
   _____

continued

Teaching Resources E • *Adventures in Appreciation*

NAME _____

CLASS _____ DATE _____   STUDY GUIDE—CONTINUED

Understanding Vocabulary

7. Determine how the following words are used in the drama. Then use each in a sentence of your own.

   a. apprehension (page 690): _____
   _____

   b. tirade (page 704): _____
   _____

   c. unperturbed (page 709): _____
   _____

   d. queue (page 714): _____
   _____

   e. commiseration (page 727): _____
   _____

Understanding Literary Elements

8. Modern drama has seen the rise of the *antihero,* a protagonist who does not exhibit the classically heroic qualities of nobility, wisdom, or moral courage. In this drama, Holly Martins well fits the porter's description of the third man: "He was just—ordinary."

   a. Describe the positive and negative qualities you see in Holly Martins. _____
   _____
   _____
   _____
   _____

   b. Did you feel at the end that Holly Martins was right to help the police and thus betray his friend? _____
   _____
   _____
   _____

continued

132 Teaching Resources E • *Adventures in Appreciation*

NAME _____

CLASS _____ DATE _____ STUDY GUIDE—CONTINUED

Writing and Responding to Literature

9. What do you imagine Harry Lime was doing when Holly Martins first saw him on the dark street? Explain why you think he had come out of hiding.

_____
_____
_____
_____
_____
_____

NAME _____

Language Skills

CLASS _____ DATE _____ SCORE _____

The Third Man *Graham Greene and Carol Reed*   (Page 689)

―――――――――― **PARALLEL STRUCTURE** ――――――――――

When two or more ideas have equal importance, writers often add clarity and smoothness by expressing the ideas in a similar manner. Notice in the following three sentences how equal ideas are similarly expressed.

> He said I was to drive you out to the airfield or take you to the bus, whichever you prefer. *(Page 698)*
>
> She goes onto the stage and, playing her first lines towards him, watches with an expression, puzzled and distressed, the stranger who has broken into her grief. *(Page 698)*
>
> Paine fetches a lantern, pulls down a sheet, and turns out the light. *(Page 718)*

By using similar grammatical constructions for equal ideas, a writer creates **parallelism.** A parallel structure is most often created with a **coordinating conjunction:** *and, but, or, nor, for, so, yet*. In the first example sentence, two infinitive phrases are joined by *or*. In the second example, two verbs and two participles are each joined by *and*. In the third example, three verbs are joined in a series using *and*.

Sentence parts joined by such conjunctions should be as grammatically equal as possible. Note that the infinitive phrases in the first sentence have the same basic structure: the infinitive plus a simple prepositional phrase. Also note that in the second sentence, the tense of the two verbs is the same; both are in present tense.

ACTIVITY A

Underline the words or groups of words joined by a coordinating conjunction in each of the following quotations. Then in the space provided, tell what kind of elements are being joined (noun phrases, verbs or predicates, participles, and so on).

1. Paine advances to meet him and holds out an envelope. *(Page 698)*

   _____

   _____

2. Above it she sees her face in the mirror with tousled hair and hopeless eyes. *(Page 701)*

   _____

   _____

continued ☞

NAME _____

CLASS _____ DATE _____   LANGUAGE SKILLS—CONTINUED

3. She opens the drawer and pulls out a comb. *(Page 701)*

_____
_____

4. She drops the comb, slams the drawer to, and puts her hand over her face. *(Page 701)*

_____
_____

5. . . . he skulks there, watching the scene, waiting his opportunity. *(Page 703)*

_____
_____

ACTIVITY B

In the space provided, rewrite each of the following sentences so that the underlined words or groups of words are grammatically equal.

EXAMPLE   Holly Martins gets off the train and walked through the barrier.

Holly Martins gets off the train and walks through the barrier.

Or

Holly Martins got off the train and walked through the barrier.

[To achieve parallelism, the verbs must have the same tense.]

6. Martins vowed to avenge his friend Harry and rescuing Anna from the police.

_____
_____

7. Martins seeks out the porter, a witness to the accident, and Dr. Winkel, who attended Harry at the accident scene.

_____
_____

continued

NAME _____

CLASS _____ DATE _____ LANGUAGE SKILLS—CONTINUED

8. Harry <u>hides</u> in the sewers, and there he <u>shot</u> Paine.

_____

_____

9. Calloway wasn't interested in whether Harry Lime was killed <u>by his friends</u> or <u>accidentally</u>.

_____

_____

10. Calloway said that Harry was <u>a racketeer</u> and <u>he murdered children</u>.

_____

_____

Repeating Words for Emphasis in Parallel Structures

For greater emphasis, a writer may make equal ideas almost exactly the same in structure by repeating certain words.

    EXAMPLE   This isn't Santa Fe, I'm not a sheriff, and you aren't a cowboy. *(Page 717)*

The negative *not* is repeated in each clause. Note also that the three equal clauses are very balanced in length and subject-verb structure. Each subject is a pronoun, and each verb is a linking verb. Used sparingly, such close parallelism can add power as well as clarity to writing.

ACTIVITY C

Underline the groups of words balanced by parallelism in each quotation. Then circle the words that are repeated for emphasis.

11. There are more crucifixes hanging on the walls and perched on the cupboards . . . than one can count, none of later date than the seventeenth century. *(Page 706)*

12. I've been frightened, I've been alone, I've been without friends and money, but I've never known anything like this. *(Page 711)*

13. Anna and Martins walk as naturally as they can, but sometimes hurrying too much, and then slowing too much. *(Page 713)*

14. So a nice trade started here. Stealing penicillin from the military hospitals, diluting it to make it go further, selling it to patients. *(Page 717)*

15. I saw him buried, and now I've seen him alive. *(Page 724)*

continued

NAME _____

CLASS _____ DATE _____   LANGUAGE SKILLS—CONTINUED

ACTIVITY D

Add words to complete each of the following sentences to balance it grammatically.

16. One passenger group gets out on the other side, and another group _____
_____

17. The Russians have their five-year plan, and I _____
_____

18. Anna, an actress, was Harry's girlfriend; Holly, _____
_____

19. Harry's personality combined a boy never grown up and _____
_____

20. I never experienced pre-war Vienna, with its Strauss music, its glamor, and its
_____

Teaching Resources E • *Adventures in Appreciation*

Building Vocabulary

NAME _____

CLASS _____ DATE _____ SCORE _____

The Third Man *Graham Greene* and *Carol Reed* (Page 689)

──────────── **DISTINGUISHING MULTIPLE MEANINGS** ────────────

A great many words in the English language have more than one meaning. The correct meaning to use for one of these words can be determined only through context.

ACTIVITY

After each of the following sentences, two meanings are given for the italicized word in the sentence. Circle the letter of the meaning that fits the context.

1. In the *Pink Panther* movies, Peter Sellers plays a bumbling detective whose *apprehension* of the guilty party is usually a matter of chance.
   a. capture or arrest **b.** dread

2. Instructions to the secret agent were to leave the *packet* of microfilm at the newsstand in the lobby.
   a. small package **b.** type of boat

3. Although the figures in the painting appear to be enjoying themselves on a spring afternoon, the work has dark, somber *undertones*.
   a. low tones of voice **b.** underlying colors

4. The *rigmarole* involved in registering for college classes has been replaced at many schools with streamlined approaches such as registration by mail or telephone.
   a. time-wasting procedures **b.** foolish talk

5. Before Joseph Lister introduced the germ theory in the 1800s, unclean conditions during surgery and *ensuing* infections were common.
   a. following immediately **b.** resulting

6. In the Soviet Union, it was not uncommon to see long *queues* for even the most common products such as shoes or light bulbs.
   a. braids or pigtails **b.** waiting lines of people

7. According to *protocol*, the President of the United States does not bow to a monarch such as the Queen of England.
   a. original draft of a document **b.** code of ceremonial forms and courtesies

8. Mary's *intention* is to attend summer school to improve her reading skills.
   a. plan **b.** determination

Selection Vocabulary Test

NAME _____

CLASS _____ DATE _____ SCORE _____

The Third Man *Graham Greene* and *Carol Reed* (Page 689)

―――――――――――――― **VOCABULARY TEST** ――――――――――――――

A. Match each word in column I with the correct definition in column II. Place the letter of each definition you choose in the space provided. (8 points each)

I	II
_____ 1. post-mortem	**a.** fussy business
_____ 2. subaltern	**b.** correct and proper procedures
_____ 3. shanghaied	**c.** long, denouncing speech
_____ 4. rigmarole	**d.** system of illegal trade
_____ 5. queue	**e.** examination after death
_____ 6. protocol	**f.** a subordinate military officer
_____ 7. meningitis	**g.** a leader, particularly a tyrant
_____ 8. Führer	**h.** compelled to do something through trickery
_____ 9. Black Market	**i.** inflammation of the membranes around the brain and spinal cord
_____ 10. tirade	**j.** a line of people

B. In the space provided, write the letter of the word or phrase closest in meaning to the italicized word. (5 points each)

_____ 1. The gloomy house filled him with *apprehension*.
(a) good feelings (b) hatred (c) dread (d) remorse

_____ 2. The prisoner did not expect any *commiseration*.
(a) sympathy (b) pain (c) gratitude (d) dinner

_____ 3. Cheryl was *unperturbed* that I brought the car back an hour late.
(a) mad (b) upset (c) not surprised (d) not upset

_____ 4. Weigh the matter carefully, and consider the consequences that will *ensue*.
(a) follow immediately (b) happen later (c) never happen (d) possibly happen

Teaching Resources E • *Adventures in Appreciation*

Selection Test

NAME _____

CLASS _____ DATE _____ SCORE _____

The Third Man Graham Greene and Carol Reed (Page 689)

Reading Comprehension. Write the letter of the *best* answer to each question. *(10 points each)*

1. The police did not arrest Lime even though they knew of his racketeering because they
   a. feared for the informant's life
   b. didn't have enough evidence to convict him
   c. didn't have enough evidence to arrest all involved
   d. feared for Anna's life   1. _____

2. The play's "third" man turned out to be
   a. Brodsky   c. Popescu
   b. Harbin   d. Lime   2. _____

3. Martins and Lime first met when they were in
   a. Vienna   c. the Casanova Club
   b. college   d. World War II   3. _____

4. Holly Martins is determined to discover the identity of the third man because he
   a. is certain the third man is Lime
   b. thinks the third man's identity will prove Lime's death was a murder and not an accident
   c. wants to prove Calloway's incompetence
   d. thinks the third man can clear Lime of any crimes   4. _____

5. Calloway accuses Lime of racketeering in murder because
   a. some of Lime's victims have died because of his crime
   b. Calloway is using hyperbole for dramatic effect
   c. Calloway wants to intimidate Martins
   d. Calloway will say anything to attack Lime's character   5. _____

6. Anna's real nationality is
   a. Austrian   c. Czechoslovakian
   b. English   d. German   6. _____

7. The scene in which Martins lectures at the cultural center is an example of
   a. plot resolution   c. comic relief
   b. plot complication   d. falling action   7. _____

8. Why does Martins agree to set up a meeting with Lime that will help Calloway capture him?
   a. To ensure his passage back to America
   b. To prevent any more murders by Lime
   c. To see that right wins out over evil
   d. To ensure Anna's freedom   8. _____

continued

140 Teaching Resources E • *Adventures in Appreciation*

NAME _____

CLASS _____ DATE _____ SELECTION TEST—CONTINUED

9. What is the Black Market item Lime is involved in selling?
   a. cigarettes   c. weapons
   b. medicine   d. whiskey   9. _____

10. The police informant whose body is found in Lime's coffin was
    a. Harbin   c. Paine
    b. Popescu   d. Kurtz   10. _____

TEACHER'S NOTES

UNIT 4: Drama

UNIT ASSESSMENT STRATEGIES

UNIT TESTS The assessment tools provided with this program include **Mastery Tests, Analogy Tests,** and **Composition Tests**. These tests, covering materials in this section, are found on the pages that follow the **Teacher's Notes**. Answer Keys for these tests begin below.

ALTERNATE OR PORTFOLIO ASSESSMENT Since students vary widely in their aptitude and learning styles, this program provides evaluation tools for a broad range of assessment strategies. The forms and guidelines in this program provide rubrics for you to use in assessing compositions or for student or peer-group evaluation of compositions.

In addition to the unit tests described above, here is a list of other evaluation or assessment tools that are in the program:

- **Student Learning Options**—These suggested unit projects are listed on the unit interleaf pages in the *Annotated Teacher's Edition*.
- **Suggestions for Portfolio Assessment Projects**—This list of possible projects for student portfolios is located in the *Portfolio Assessment and Professional Support Materials* booklet.
- **Fine Arts and Instructional Transparencies**—These transparencies reinforce concepts covered in the unit. The transparencies are accompanied by Teacher's Notes and blackline masters with writing skills. The transparencies for each unit are located in the *Audiovisual Resource Binder*.
- **Evaluation Guides**—These forms are helpful for revising and assessing student papers, whether by you as instructor, by the student, or by peer evaluators. See the *Portfolio Assessment and Professional Support Materials* booklet.

For a variety of assessment and evaluation suggestions, see the *Portfolio Assessment and Professional Support Materials* booklet.

ANSWER KEYS

MASTERY TEST A

Drama: Understanding the Selections

A. 1. b   5. a
    2. a   6. c
    3. b   7. b
    4. c   8. b

B. 9. e   14. c
    10. f   15. d
    11. b   16. f
    12. a   17. e
    13. c   18. a

C. **For Composition**
Guidelines for Essay Topic
In a well-written essay on this topic, the student should:

1. Reflect an accurate understanding of the assignment
2. For each play the student should:
   - Identify the play under discussion
   - Identify the hero or heroine and the inescapable situation
   - Discuss choices leading to the situation
3. Support all generalizations with details from the selected plays
4. Demonstrate effective use of the following writing skills:
   - Vocabulary
   - Mechanics (spelling/punctuation/grammar)
   - Sentence structure
   - Organization (logical arrangement of ideas)

continued

MASTERY TEST B

Drama: Applying Literature Skills

A. 1. a
 2. d
 3. a
 4. b
 5. c
 6. d
 7. c

B. 8. c
 9. c
 10. a
 11. b
 12. a
 13. d
 14. d
 15. d
 16. a
 17. a

ANALOGY TEST A

1. —C— vexed : outraged :: appreciative : adoring
 Vexed (irritated) differs in degree from outraged in a similar way that appreciative differs from adoring.
2. —B— flint : fire :: ignition : vehicle
 A flint is a small stone used to start a fire. An ignition is used to start a vehicle.
3. —A— disperse : assemble :: dote : dislike
 Disperse (to scatter in various directions) is an antonym of assemble just as dote (like excessively) is an antonym of dislike.
4. —C— tolerable : tolerate :: retentive : retain
 Tolerable and retentive are adjective forms of the verbs tolerate and retain.
5. —D— greeting : salutation :: belongings : possessions
 Greeting is a synonym of salutation just as belongings is a synonym of possessions.
6. —B— exam : apprehension :: favor : gratitude
 An exam causes apprehension (dread) just as a favor causes gratitude.
7. —E— eager : avid :: reflective : thoughtful
 Eager is a synonym of avid just as reflective is a synonym of thoughtful.
8. —D— conceived : wrought :: rehearsed : performed
 In a time sequence, something is conceived (thought of) before it is wrought (created) in a similar way that a play is rehearsed before it is performed.
9. —D— phantasm : unreal :: music : rhythmic
 Being unreal is a characteristic of a phantasm (phantom) just as being rhythmic is a characteristic of music.
10. —A— surreptitious : conspicuous :: peculiar : normal
 Surreptitious (secret) is an antonym of conspicuous just as peculiar is an antonym of normal.
11. —C— augurer : predict :: ax : hew
 An augurer is someone who predicts the future from signs or omens. An ax is something used to hew (chop) wood.
12. —B— ripping : rent :: piling : stack
 Ripping causes a rent (a hole or opening) in something. Piling causes a stack to form.
13. —A— lecture : tirade :: squirt : gush
 Lecture differs in degree from tirade (a long, vehement, or denouncing speech) in a similar way that squirt differs from gush.
14. —D— dirge : music :: directory : list
 A dirge (funeral hymn) is a type of music just as a directory is a type of list.
15. —C— nondescript : distinguished :: meek : defiant
 Nondescript (not having any distinguishing qualities or characteristics) is an antonym of distinguished just as meek (timid) is an antonym of defiant.
16. —E— slavish : servile :: continuous : ceaseless
 Slavish is a synonym of servile (submissive) just as continuous is a synonym of ceaseless.
17. —A— dancer : lithe :: runt : scrawny
 Being lithe (easily graceful; limber) is characteristic of a dancer just as being scrawny (thin and weak) is characteristic of a runt (the smallest animal of a litter).
18. —C— shield : deflect :: telescope : magnify
 A shield deflects (turns aside blows) in a similar way that a telescope magnifies.
19. —D— entrails : liver :: sentence : verb
 The liver is part of the entrails (internal organs) of a human or animal. A verb is part of a sentence.
20. —B— prodigious : minute :: listless : energetic
 Prodigious (enormous) is an antonym of minute (tiny) just as listless (lacking energy) is an antonym of energetic.

ANALOGY TEST B

1. —A— origin : terminus :: construction : demolition
 In a time sequence, the origin comes before the terminus (final point) just as construction comes before demolition.
2. —B— ludicrous : absurd :: base : dishonorable
 Ludicrous (ridiculous) is a synonym of absurd just as base is a synonym of dishonorable.
3. —C— crest : hill :: climax : story
 The crest is the peak or highest point of a hill just as the climax is the highest point of a story.
4. —E— plow : till :: yoke : harness
 A plow is used to till (cultivate) land. A yoke is a wooden bar fitted around the necks of a pair of work animals and used to harness them together.
5. —B— interpret : construe :: mollify : soothe
 Interpret is a synonym of construe just as mollify is a synonym of soothe.

continued

6. —D— canyon : crevice :: hurricane : drizzle
A canyon differs in degree from a crevice (a narrow crack) just as a hurricane differs from a drizzle.

7. —A— hostility : geniality :: confidence : insecurity
Hostility is an antonym of geniality (friendliness) just as confidence is an antonym of insecurity.

8. —A— seduce : seduction :: motivate : motivation
Seduce and motivate are verb forms of the nouns seduction and motivation.

9. —E— incongruous : suitable :: melodramatic : unemotional
Incongruous (lacking in suitability, harmony, or logic) is an antonym of suitable just as melodramatic (overly emotional) is an antonym of unemotional.

10. —C— blasphemy : irreverence :: boasting : pride
Irreverence (lack of respect, love, or awe for something sacred) is characterized by blasphemy (any contemptuous act or remark). Pride is characterized by boasting.

11. —D— proletariat : class :: dirge : song
The proletariat (working people) is a type of social class. A dirge is a type of song.

12. —B— conference : parley :: quarrel : dispute
Conference is a synonym of parley just as quarrel is a synonym of dispute.

13. —A— starve : emaciated :: borrow : indebted
Starving causes one to become emaciated (abnormally thin). Borrowing causes one to become indebted.

14. —E— eulogy : praise :: prediction : foretell
A eulogy (speech delivered at a funeral) praises the deceased person. A prediction foretells an event that is about to happen.

15. —D— apartment : building :: flower : garland
An apartment is part of a building just as a flower is part of a garland (a wreath of flowers and ribbons).

16. —C— dowager : elderly :: impostor : dishonest
Being elderly is characteristic of a dowager (a well-to-do, elderly woman, especially a widow). Being dishonest is characteristic of an impostor (someone who deceives or cheats others).

17. —E— covert : hidden :: friendly : affable
Covert is a synonym of hidden just as friendly is a synonym of affable.

18. —A— chide : revile :: irritate : exasperate
Chide (to scold mildly) differs in degree from revile (to abuse verbally; to insult) in a similar way that irritate differs from exasperate (annoy greatly).

19. —C— corpse : carrion :: hay : fodder
A corpse becomes carrion (food for animals that eat decayed flesh) just as hay becomes fodder (food for livestock).

20. —B— sinew : anatomy :: mayor : government
A sinew (tendon) is part of one's anatomy (structure of an organism) just as a mayor is a part of government.

COMPOSITION TEST

Student answers will vary, but students should write a composition response that has coherence and unity and that adequately covers the topic selected. Students should select a topic from among the choices given, express their opinions clearly in accordance with materials that they have read, and support their ideas with quotations or specific details from the selections. You may want to have students evaluate one another's compositions in cooperative groups. For assessment, you may wish to use one of the array of evaluation guides in the *Portfolio Assessment and Professional Support Materials* booklet.

MASTERY TEST A

NAME _____

CLASS _____ DATE _____ SCORE _____

DRAMA

Understanding the Selections

A. Reading Comprehension. Write the letter of the *best* answer to each question. *(5 points each)*

1. In *Antigone*, the title character does which of the following?
   a. Defies her father about a marriage, then kills herself
   b. Defies an edict in order to perform an act of love and piety
   c. Supports her fiancé in his defiance of his father
   d. Breaks a sacred law and is punished by the gods   1. _____

2. To understand fully the action and meaning of *Antigone,* we must remember that it is about the ruling family of Thebes and a(n)
   a. curse on the house
   b. long tradition of tyranny and hatred of tyranny
   c. quarrel between rival gods
   d. ancient war between Thebes and another city   2. _____

3. Considered as a whole, *Julius Caesar* essentially is a
   a. vivid "spectacle" play
   b. study in the characters of great men
   c. dramatized history of Rome
   d. study of a great man's secret weakness   3. _____

4. Which of the following *incorrectly* matches an important aspect of the play and an event or moment?
   a. Foreshadowing: the appearance of Caesar's ghost in Brutus' tent
   b. Turning point: the populace's response to Antony's oration
   c. Comic relief: Antony trying to hand Caesar a crown
   d. Internal conflict: Brutus' struggle with himself before joining the conspirators   4. _____

5. *I Never Sang for My Father* can best be identified as a play with something relevant to say about
   a. relationships between people
   b. human courage and strength
   c. the brutality of modern society
   d. the generation gap   5. _____

6. As a modern drama, *I Never Sang for My Father* is most unconventional in its
   a. dialogue
   b. use of unspoken thoughts and feelings
   c. handling of scene shifts
   d. avoidance of crowd scenes   6. _____

continued

Teaching Resources E • *Adventures in Appreciation*

NAME _____

CLASS _____ DATE _____ MASTERY TEST A—CONTINUED

7. *The Third Man* is a drama that involves a conflict between
   a. two brothers who have different philosophies of life
   b. loyalty to a friend and loyalty to justice
   c. loyalty to a friend and love for a woman
   d. upholding the law and saving a life   7. _____

8. *The Third Man* relies on which one of the following elements to create suspense?
   a. Dialogue   c. Sound effects
   b. Camera effects   d. Fist fights   8. _____

B. Identifying Characters. The following two sets of questions require you to match a character with a statement or comment that he or she makes. Use an answer only once. (*6 points each*)

   a. Creon   d. Brutus
   b. Antigone   e. Caesar
   c. Cassius   f. Portia

9. "Cowards die many times before their deaths,
   The valiant never taste of death but once."   9. _____

10. "You have some sick offense within your mind,
    Which by the right and virtue of my place
    I ought to know of."   10. _____

11.   ". . . Leave me my foolish plan:
    I am not afraid of the danger; if it means death,
    I will not be the worst of death—death without honor."   11. _____

12.   ". . . I'll have no dealings
    With lawbreakers, critics of the government:
    Whoever is chosen to govern should be obeyed—
    Must be obeyed, in all things, great and small. . . ."   12. _____

13. "Tis better that the enemy seek us.
    So shall he waste his means, weary his soldiers,
    Doing himself offense, whilst we lying still
    Are full of rest, defense, and nimbleness."   13. _____

   a. Harry   d. Tom Garrison
   b. Crabbit   e. Gene Garrison
   c. Anna   f. Margaret Garrison

14. ". . . I don't know anything anymore except . . . I want to be dead too."   14. _____

15. "Well, I'm certainly glad you're here. My mind's like a sieve. . . . It's the confusion and worrying. . . ."   15. _____

16. "A new place, a new wife, a new life. I would feel just terrible if you didn't go because of me."   16. _____

continued

146 Teaching Resources E • *Adventures in Appreciation*

NAME _____

CLASS _____ DATE _____ MASTERY TEST A—CONTINUED

17. "What do you want for gratitude? Nothing, nothing would be enough. You have resented everything you ever gave me. The orphan boy in you has resented everything."   17. _____

18. "In Switzerland they had brotherly love, five hundred years of democracy and peace, and what did that produce . . . ? The cuckoo clock."   18. _____

C. For Composition. "Tragedy requires that the hero or heroine make choices that lead to a situation from which there is no escape" (page 478). Show how this statement applies to *Antigone, Julius Caesar,* and *I Never Sang for My Father.*

Mastery Test B

NAME _____

CLASS _____ DATE _____ SCORE _____

DRAMA

Applying Literature Skills

A. Comparing Excerpts. Following are excerpts taken from two plays, one by Shakespeare, one by an American playwright. Read each excerpt carefully, and then answer the questions that follow. (*10 points each*)

Excerpt 1

      Scene 12, Hills adjoining to Alexandria
       [*Enter* Antony *and* Scarus.]

Antony. Yet they are not joined. Where yond pine does stand,
 I shall discover all: I'll bring thee word
 Straight, how 'tis like to go.   [*Exit.*]
Scarus.   Swallows have built
 In Cleopatra's sails their nests. The augurers[1]
 Say they know not, they cannot tell, look grimly,   5
 And dare not speak their knowledge. Antony
 Is valiant, and dejected, and by starts
 His fretted[2] fortunes give him hope, and fear,
 Of what he has, and has not.   [*Alarum afar off, as at a seafight.*]
      [*Re-enter* Antony.]
Antony.   All is lost;
 This foul Egyptian hath betrayed me.   10
 My fleet hath yielded to the foe, and yonder
 They cast their caps up and carouse together
 Like friends long lost. . . .
     —William Shakespeare, *Antony and Cleopatra,* Act Four

Excerpt 2

"The Liddy Ann in a Sou'easter"
 (Note: *The storm noises are well worked up before the scene opens. The stage is completely dark, as is the front of the theater.*)
 Scene: *An expanse of wild, storm-tossed waves, with the lighthouse, a dark, shadowy bulk, rising from the rocky coast on the left. The rain is pouring in torrents, the thunder roars, the lightning flashes. The boom of a ship's gun is heard above the din of the storm, and in the darkness, the* Liddy Ann, *sloop-rigged and under reefed jib, makes her way slowly through the heavy seas, from right to left. She is off her course and perilously near the rocks. At intervals her gun booms and she sends up distress signals. The figures of* Captain Ben, Dave Burgess, Gabe Kilpatrick, *and* Bill Hodgekins, *as well as* Sam *and* Helen, *can be dimly discerned on board. The shouts of* Captain Ben *giving orders, and the replies of the crew are drowned by the noise of the storm.*

---

1. **augurers** (ô′gy-rz): officials who made predictions from omens
2. **fretted:** worn

continued ☞

148   Teaching Resources E   •   *Adventures in Appreciation*

NAME _____

CLASS _____ DATE _____   MASTERY TEST B—CONTINUED

> For a few moments the *Liddy Ann tosses helplessly in the darkness. Then a tiny light appears in the lowest window of the lighthouse. For a second it wavers, then slowly it rises from window to window, as* Uncle Nat *climbs the stairs to the tower. In another moment the light in the tower blazes forth, showing the* Liddy Ann *her course. A shout of relief goes up from those on the boat, and as the* Liddy Ann *makes her way safely past the rocks.*
> *The Curtain Descends*
> —James A. Herne, *Shore Acres*, Act Three, Scene 2

1. In which excerpt can we detect an obvious use of foreshadowing?
   a. Excerpt 1 only
   b. Excerpt 2 only
   c. Both excerpts
   d. Neither excerpt   1. _____

2. Which excerpt contains a soliloquy?
   a. Excerpt 1 only
   b. Excerpt 2 only
   c. Both excerpts
   d. Neither excerpt   2. _____

3. The dramatist of which excerpt clearly found it impossible to produce on stage a naval scene?
   a. Excerpt 1 only
   b. Excerpt 2 only
   c. Both excerpts
   d. Neither excerpt   3. _____

4. Which excerpt would be difficult to produce on the stage of a theater-in-the-round?
   a. Excerpt 1 only
   b. Excerpt 2 only
   c. Both excerpts
   d. Neither excerpt   4. _____

5. Which excerpt makes obvious use of special sound effects?
   a. Excerpt 1 only
   b. Excerpt 2 only
   c. Both excerpts
   d. Neither excerpt   5. _____

6. Which excerpt asks the impossible of even a resourceful stage director?
   a. Excerpt 1 only
   b. Excerpt 2 only
   c. Both excerpts
   d. Neither excerpt   6. _____

7. Which excerpt concerns itself with a moment of peril?
   a. Excerpt 1 only
   b. Excerpt 2 only
   c. Both excerpts
   d. Neither excerpt   7. _____

B. Understanding Dramatic Technique. Write the letter of the *best* answer to each question. *(3 points each)*

8. In the excerpt from *Antony and Cleopatra*, Scarus' one speech tells us that the Egyptian fleet is
   a. a very large one
   b. a very old one
   c. reluctant to sail
   d. waiting for a favorable wind   8. _____

9. In this speech, Shakespeare has Scarus using
   a. a generalization
   b. a riddle
   c. contrast
   d. foreshadowing   9. _____

continued

NAME _____

CLASS _____ DATE _____   MASTERY TEST B—CONTINUED

10. The single word *Alarum* can best be identified as a
    a. stage direction for sound effects
    b. signal to drop a curtain
    c. signal to produce crowd noises
    d. stage direction to begin an onstage battle   10. _____

11. We can assume that the period of time elapsing between Antony's exit and his return on stage is about
    a. five seconds   c. four or five minutes
    b. a minute or less   d. ten minutes   11. _____

12. The *Shore Acres* excerpt can best be identified as
    a. lengthy stage directions   c. an introduction
    b. a prologue   d. a grand finale   12. _____

13. The excerpt from *Shore Acres* utilizes all of the following sound effects *except*
    a. thunder
    b. shouts of sailors
    c. a signal gun
    d. shouted directions from a lighthouse   13. _____

14. In a theater, the effect of the *Shore Acres* excerpt would depend *least* on
    a. lighting effects   c. movements of the actors
    b. sound effects   d. dialogue   14. _____

15. The scene from *Shore Acres* is performed in
    a. complete darkness throughout
    b. enough artificial light to allow visibility
    c. normal stage lighting
    d. realistic darkness relieved by lightning   15. _____

16. Presumably, the words shouted by the crew of the *Liddy Ann* are
    a. completely drowned out
    b. loud and clear
    c. intended to be heard by the audience
    d. pantomimed, not spoken   16. _____

17. This excerpt from *Shore Acres* can best be described as
    a. an exciting, suspenseful scene
    b. a pantomime skit
    c. a typical piece of realistic drama
    d. a satire on realistic drama   17. _____

150 Teaching Resources E • *Adventures in Appreciation*

Analogy Test A

NAME _____

CLASS _____ DATE _____ SCORE _____

DRAMA

Analogies. Determine the relationship between the capitalized words in each of the following numbered items; then find a pair of words within the answer choices having the same relationship. Use test sentences to try all choices before deciding upon the correct answer. Write the letter of your choice in the space provided.

QUESTION 1 _____
VEXED : OUTRAGED ::
A. shaded : shadowy
B. fawning : licking
C. appreciative : adoring
D. example : copy
E. whip : cow

QUESTION 2 _____
FLINT : FIRE ::
A. heirloom : legacy
B. ignition : vehicle
C. narrow : deep
D. escape : capture
E. decree : order

QUESTION 3 _____
DISPERSE : ASSEMBLE ::
A. dote : dislike
B. moral : virtuous
C. groove : tunnel
D. crowd : outward
E. disconsolate : unhappy

QUESTION 4 _____
TOLERABLE : TOLERATE ::
A. appoint : opposite
B. counsel : council
C. retentive : retain
D. burial : cremation
E. unable : relative

QUESTION 5 _____
GREETING : SALUTATION ::
A. tightly : stretched
B. auspicious : mistrusting
C. immortal : undying
D. belongings : possessions
E. crowded : noisier

QUESTION 6 _____
EXAM : APPREHENSION ::
A. daydream : boredom
B. favor : gratitude
C. error : correction
D. rheumy : watery
E. sudden : automatic

QUESTION 7 _____
EAGER : AVID ::
A. lengthen : measure
B. deference : polite
C. rubbery : jumpy
D. prejudice : injustice
E. reflective : thoughtful

QUESTION 8 _____
CONCEIVED : WROUGHT ::
A. citadel : defend
B. simmer : broil
C. depth : surface
D. rehearsed : performed
E. pronounce : announce

QUESTION 9 _____
PHANTASM : UNREAL ::
A. wrack : torture
B. isolated : empty
C. complicated : details
D. music : rhythmic
E. relax : sedative

QUESTION 10 _____
SURREPTITIOUS : CONSPICUOUS ::
A. peculiar : normal
B. sharpen : whetstone
C. solicitude : isolation
D. ambition : display
E. permanent : enduring

continued

ANALOGY TEST A—CONTINUED

QUESTION 11 _____
AUGURER : PREDICT ::
A. clapping : applause
B. chapter : book
C. ax : hew
D. mask : concealment
E. hero : valor

QUESTION 12 _____
RIPPING : RENT ::
A. scavenging : hobo
B. piling : stack
C. secretive : sly
D. damp : dank
E. crossing : bridge

QUESTION 13 _____
LECTURE : TIRADE ::
A. squirt : gush
B. pattern : model
C. senile : forgetful
D. furthest : utmost
E. papers : documents

QUESTION 14 _____
DIRGE : MUSIC ::
A. former : previous
B. elocution : penalty
C. rite : wedding
D. directory : list
E. faith : religion

QUESTION 15 _____
NONDESCRIPT : DISTINGUISHED ::
A. resentment : pique
B. pinion : belief
C. meek : defiant
D. guidance : steerage
E. credible : practical

QUESTION 16 _____
SLAVISH : SERVILE ::
A. nothing : aught
B. customs : regulations
C. concave : cavernous
D. grudge : revenge
E. continuous : ceaseless

QUESTION 17 _____
DANCER : LITHE ::
A. runt : scrawny
B. demonstration : riot
C. phase : interim
D. beg : entreat
E. box : carton

QUESTION 18 _____
SHIELD : DEFLECT ::
A. gradually : instantly
B. monologue : speech
C. telescope : magnify
D. agreement : harmony
E. conjoint : bend

QUESTION 19 _____
ENTRAILS : LIVER ::
A. woven : pattern
B. dodder : food
C. patient : forbearing
D. sentence : verb
E. journey : step

QUESTION 20 _____
PRODIGIOUS : MINUTE ::
A. inward : centripetal
B. listless : energetic
C. infused : refused
D. glimmer : healer
E. fort : fortress

Analogy Test B

NAME _____
CLASS _____ DATE _____ SCORE _____

DRAMA

Analogies. Determine the relationship between the capitalized words in each of the following numbered items; then find a pair of words within the answer choices having the same relationship. Use test sentences to try all choices before deciding upon the correct answer. Write the letter of your choice in the space provided.

QUESTION 1 _____
ORIGIN : TERMINUS ::
A. construction : demolition
B. episode : movie
C. susceptible : victim
D. nonsense : foolish
E. ornament : customary

QUESTION 2 _____
LUDICROUS : ABSURD ::
A. protection : guard
B. base : dishonorable
C. peaceful : disturbance
D. persistent : uncertain
E. discourse : unassigned

QUESTION 3 _____
CREST : HILL ::
A. apparition : ghost
B. mischief : prank
C. climax : story
D. infant : teen-ager
E. street : curb

QUESTION 4 _____
PLOW : TILL ::
A. residence : home
B. hollow : solid
C. society : nation
D. will : executor
E. yoke : harness

QUESTION 5 _____
INTERPRET : CONSTRUE ::
A. platform : departure
B. mollify : soothe
C. affectionate : cold
D. hungry : sated
E. warm : sizzling

QUESTION 6 _____
CANYON : CREVICE ::
A. waste : desert
B. contradict : admit
C. profane : contempt
D. hurricane : drizzle
E. astounded : startled

QUESTION 7 _____
HOSTILITY : GENIALITY ::
A. confidence : insecurity
B. very : extremely
C. rumor : scandal
D. boating : recreation
E. exalted : sublime

QUESTION 8 _____
SEDUCE : SEDUCTION ::
A. motivate : motivation
B. flatter : sycophant
C. construction : construct
D. hairless : hairlessness
E. adverse : adversity

QUESTION 9 _____
INCONGRUOUS : SUITABLE ::
A. recollect : assemble
B. appertain : fearful
C. kindle : fire
D. senile : forgetful
E. melodramatic : unemotional

QUESTION 10 _____
BLASPHEMY : IRREVERENCE ::
A. masterly : expert
B. significant : trivial
C. boasting : pride
D. substitute : secondary
E. decision : rational

continued

Teaching Resources E • *Adventures in Appreciation*

ANALOGY TEST B—CONTINUED

QUESTION 11 _____
PROLETARIAT : CLASS ::
A. lighting : candle
B. invasion : war
C. attendant : polite
D. dirge : song
E. substantial : large

QUESTION 12 _____
CONFERENCE : PARLEY ::
A. controversy : harmony
B. quarrel : dispute
C. dismember : forget
D. steadfast : unstable
E. step : staircase

QUESTION 13 _____
STARVE : EMACIATED ::
A. borrow : indebted
B. slavery : bondage
C. condemn : pardon
D. render : deliver
E. bereaved : funeral

QUESTION 14 _____
EULOGY : PRAISE ::
A. stylish : dowdy
B. engender : produce
C. divide : categories
D. contest : trophy
E. prediction : foretell

QUESTION 15 _____
APARTMENT : BUILDING ::
A. tremble : quiver
B. systematic : random
C. plastic : celluloid
D. flower : garland
E. portion : location

QUESTION 16 _____
DOWAGER : ELDERLY ::
A. legion : inscription
B. wrestling : rioting
C. impostor : dishonest
D. jailer : warden
E. author : profession

QUESTION 17 _____
COVERT : HIDDEN ::
A. optional : required
B. pilgrimage : traveling
C. speck : blemish
D. scale : weighing
E. friendly : affable

QUESTION 18 _____
CHIDE : REVILE ::
A. irritate : exasperate
B. betrayal : disloyalty
C. wealthy : comfortable
D. idea : conception
E. bridle : grooming

QUESTION 19 _____
CORPSE : CARRION ::
A. manage : carnage
B. death : dismay
C. hay : fodder
D. carcass : fracas
E. grave : burial

QUESTION 20 _____
SINEW : ANATOMY ::
A. purger : falsehood
B. mayor : government
C. climate : atmosphere
D. geography : frontier
E. appease : satisfy

154 Teaching Resources E • *Adventures in Appreciation*

Composition Test

NAME _____

CLASS _____ DATE _____ SCORE _____

Drama

Antigone	*Sophocles*	*(Page 494)*
Julius Caesar	*William Shakespeare*	*(Page 543)*
I Never Sang for My Father	*Robert Anderson*	*(Page 642)*
The Third Man	*Graham Greene and Carol Reed*	*(Page 689)*

A. The most important element in drama is *conflict*. Choose one of the plays listed above, and in a brief essay, show how the conflict is developed and how it is resolved.

B. Discuss the conventions of Shakespeare's theater, referring to *Julius Caesar* for specific examples of each feature. Include the following: the use of prose and verse, the soliloquy, the aside, costumes, and staging.

C. Who is the protagonist, or central figure, in *Julius Caesar?* Before coming to a conclusion, reread the comments on page 637 of your textbook. Write an essay defending your answer.

D. *Verbal irony* occurs when a character says one thing and means another. *Irony of situation* occurs when a situation turns out contrary to our expectations. *Dramatic irony* occurs when the reader or a member of the audience knows something that a character is not aware of. Choose *one* kind of irony and demonstrate its significance in any of the plays listed above.

E. The *theme* of a play is its central meaning—the insight it provides into life or human nature. State the theme of *I Never Sang for My Father*.

_____
_____
_____
_____
_____
_____
_____
_____
_____

continued

Teaching Resources E • Adventures in Appreciation

NAME _____

CLASS _____ DATE _____ COMPOSITION TEST—CONTINUED

AUDIO-VISUAL CENTER
MISSOURI SOUTHERN STATE COLLEGE